M000296318

Empowering the Voice of the Teacher Researcher

Achieving Success through a Culture of Inquiry

Edited by
Roger Brindley and Christine Crocco

ROWMAN & LITTLEFIELD EDUCATION
A division of
ROWMAN & LITTLEFIELD PUBLISHERS, INC.
Lanham • New York • Toronto • Plymouth, UK

Published by Rowman & Littlefield Education
A division of Rowman & Littlefield Publishers, Inc.
A wholly owned subsidiary of The Rowman & Littlefield Publishing Group, Inc.
4501 Forbes Boulevard, Suite 200, Lanham, Maryland 20706
http://www.rowmaneducation.com

Estover Road, Plymouth PL6 7PY, United Kingdom

Copyright © 2009 by Roger Brindley and Christine Crocco

All rights reserved. No part of this book may be reproduced in any form or by any electronic or mechanical means, including information storage and retrieval systems, without written permission from the publisher, except by a reviewer who may quote passages in a review.

British Library Cataloguing in Publication Information Available

Library of Congress Cataloging-in-Publication Data

Empowering the voice of the teacher researcher : achieving success through a culture of inquiry / edited by Roger Brindley and Christine Crocco.
    p. cm.
  Includes bibliographical references.
  ISBN 978-1-60709-966-6 (cloth : alk. paper) -- ISBN 978-1-60709-967-3 (pbk. : alk. paper) -- ISBN 978-1-60709-968-0 (electronic)
  1. Action research in education--United States. I. Brindley, Roger, 1962- II. Crocco, Christine, 1951-
  LB1028.24.E556 2010
  370.72--dc22

                                                                2010035733

∞™ The paper used in this publication meets the minimum requirements of American National Standard for Information Sciences—Permanence of Paper for Printed Library Materials, ANSI/NISO Z39.48-1992. Printed in the United States of America

Contents

Part IV: Affirming the Voice of the Teacher Researcher

Foreword

Nancy Fichtman Dana

If you have ever been an *American Idol* fan, you have watched the renowned judge Simon Cowell tell contestants week after week that in order to be successful, what they must do is take a song that was written and recorded years ago and make it "contemporary," "relevant," and "something you could hear on the radio today." *Empowering the Voice of the Teacher Researcher: Achieving Success through a Culture of Inquiry* does for action research what Simon Cowell's advice does for aspiring recording artists today.

The concept of action research has been around for ages, with roots in the work of John Dewey in the 1930s, popularized by Kurt Lewin in the 1940s, and shortly thereafter applied to the field of education by Stephen Corey in the 1950s. Roger Brindley and Chris Crocco's book has given this classic school improvement and professional development process a contemporary and relevant feel and, with the help of their principal and teacher chapter authors, demonstrates the ways this powerful process could be "something you could see going on in schools today."

The first way Brindley and Crocco's book contemporizes the process of action research is by highlighting the linkages between action research and perhaps the most rapidly growing professional development phenomenon to sweep the county in the past decade—professional learning communities or PLCs.

Diane Yendol-Hoppey and I wrote about the ways PLCs and teacher research often exist and operate independently of one another in *The Reflective Educator's Guide to Professional Development: Coaching Inquiry-Oriented Learning Communities*. We suggested that these two prevalent and powerful mechanisms for teacher learning can enhance each other and therefore "magnify already powerful professional development practices occurring in many schools and districts across the nation" (Dana & Yendol-Hoppey, 2008, 11). Brindley and Crocco's book provides real stories that illustrate the results of weaving learning community and action research work together into the fabric of one school's improvement efforts.

Speaking of one school's quest to improve and become the best it can be, the second way Brindley and Crocco's book contemporizes the process of action research is by offering a collection of action research stories that are all completed in the same school. In the past few decades, there have been a number of action research collections published that have been authored by teachers, but the editors of almost all of these texts focused on finding pieces that can serve as exemplars.

To these ends, editors have combed different schools, different districts, and, in some cases, different parts of the world to find the very best examples of teacher research. Hence, the current collections we have are not always a true representation of the ways this process might play out across many teachers at a single school site as an approach to schoolwide improvement, and candid, real stories of the process, such as that offered by Danielle Lawrence in chapter 7, are lost. Brindley and Crocco's text offers a real, honest, and open account of the scope of teacher research that might occur when a school is just getting started on the inquiry journey.

A third way Brindley and Crocco's book contemporizes the action research process is by highlighting the importance of administration. In *Leading with Passion and Knowledge: The Principal as Action Researcher* (Dana, 2009), I described the ways the process of action research often utilized with teachers can be applied to a principal's study of his or her own administrative practice, but gave less attention to the ways a principal can support his or her teachers in their own individual research endeavors.

By including a full chapter entitled "The Perspectives of a School Administration" by principal and assistant principal Chris Christoff and Matt Gruhl in their book, Brindley and Crocco demonstrate how the critical support needed for action research to flourish in a school can be actualized by the administration.

The final way Brindley and Crocco's book makes the process of action research particularly relevant to today's schools is by offering a collection of teacher research from the middle school context. As these action research stories take place right "in the middle" of our educational K–12 schooling system, the action research stories shared in this book will resonate with educators at every grade level. In particular, entering into the action research cycle of reflection and self-improvement is particularly critical for the middle level educator, as meeting the unique and ever-changing needs of young adolescents will always remain a moving target for teachers due to the energy, passion, adventurousness, romanticism, risk-taking, and exploration that characterizes this age group (Sizer & Meier, 2006).

Middle school teachers know that their students' focus and moods can change not just day to day, but hour to hour. Hence, to successfully address the needs of the middle level student, middle level teachers must constantly be evolving in their teaching. What we learn from *Empowering the Voice of the Teacher Researcher: Achieving Success through a Culture of Inquiry* is that engagement in action research is a fine way to evolve not only for the middle level teacher, but for all educators!

In closing, what is most important to remember as you read this text, is that the examples of action research provided in this book demonstrate teachers who took charge of their own learning by naming and studying real problems of practice that emerged from within the four walls of their classrooms. This approach to professional development stands in stark contrast to traditional forms of professional development focused on bringing an outside "expert" into a school or district for a day to deliver information on the latest best practice. Rather than an outside expert telling administrators and teachers what they should be doing *to* students, through engagement in action research, teachers and administrators learn *with* students, engaging in a cycle of continuous reflection leading to self- and school improvement, truly becoming the best that they can be! This book celebrates that process. Congratulations to the authors!

REFERENCES

Dana, N. F. (2009). *Leading with Passion and Knowledge: The Principal as Action Researcher*. Thousand Oaks, CA: Corwin Press.

Dana, N. F., & Yendol-Hoppey, D. (2008). *The Reflective Educator's Guide to Professional Development: Coaching Inquiry-Oriented Learning Communities*. Thousand Oaks, CA: Corwin Press.

Sizer, T., & Meier, D. (2006). Foreword. In the Education Alliance at Brown University and EEI Communications (Eds.), *Breaking Ranks in the Middle: Strategies for Leading Middle Level Reform* (vii–viii). Reston, VA: National Association for Secondary Principals.

Acknowledgments

It was a privilege to write for and serve as the editors for this book. As strong advocates for teachers as professional decision makers, when we observed the administrators and teachers of Seven Springs Middle School (SSMS) acquiring the practices of community and inquiry through a deliberate and developmental process, we knew that this was a story that must be told. We are enormously grateful to these dedicated educators for their willingness to open their thinking to us and our readers.

One of the rewards of the teaching profession is that it encourages the desire to continuously learn and grow throughout one's career. The reflective nature of their stories and the steps the authors describe as they made their journey inspire all of us who partake in such a journey. In this book we celebrate the work of Chris Christoff, Lisa Fisher, Leslie Frick, Matt Gruhl, Danielle Lawrence, Cindy Tehan, Janet Tolson, Karen Wood, and Karen Zantop.

These teachers and administrators, however, represent a much broader community of educators dedicated to improving the quality of education across Seven Springs Middle School, and we wish to acknowledge all the teachers, administrators, staff, and students at SSMS who have contributed to the collaborative culture of this school, and by extension to this book.

We must also express our gratitude to colleagues who gave of their valuable time to read the draft text and offer us valuable insights that pushed our thinking deeper. Marilyn Katzenmeyer, Nancy Fichtman Dana, and Diane Yendol-Hoppey are brilliant teachers and authors whose work we greatly respect, and whose ideas shaped this book.

Marilyn is currently the president of Professional Development Center, Inc., and her expertise and guidance in the leadership arena have been instrumental to the careers of many. Nancy, professor of education and director of the Center for School Improvement at the University of Florida, and Diane, professor of education and chair of the Department of Childhood Education and Literacy at the University of South Florida, are co-authors and renowned for their work with professional development schools, teacher inquiry, and leadership.

That these remarkable mentors would agree to be our critical friends was an honor we cherish. Our thanks would not be complete without recognizing the support of Tom Koerner at Rowman and Littlefield. Like many texts, this book represents a labor of love that has come together over time. At every turn Tom has been supportive, thoughtful, and gracious in his comments, and we sincerely appreciate his editorship.

We also owe a particular debt of gratitude to Dr. Nancy Dana for writing the foreword to this book. For many years we have been avid readers of her professional texts and have viewed her as a grounded visionary, someone with both the capacity to articulate principles that will improve the teaching profession and the understanding of day-to-day education to put that vision into practice. It is a great pleasure to thank Nancy for her support.

At the heart of this effort was the love and support of our families, who understood the time and sacrifice it took to finish this book. We reserve our greatest thanks for Toni and Danny. This is for them, and for our children and grandchildren. May they always have teachers like the ones who helped write this book—teachers who continually seek to challenge themselves to share their gifts and talents and are not satisfied until they have reached every child.

Finally, this book is for teachers everywhere. Never underestimate your capacity to influence a young mind and shape the next generation. We hope, above all else, this book offers you the agency to keep high expectations for this profession, to extend your work further, and to fly upward and onward!

I

EXPLORING THE KEY CONCEPTS

Promoting Teachers as Thoughtful, Proactive and Effective Decision Makers!

Roger Brindley and Christine Crocco

In order to create a cohesive community and a consensus on how to proceed, school people must have the occasion to engage in democratic discourse about the real stuff of teaching and learning.

—Linda Darling-Hammond, *The Right to Learn:*
A Blueprint for Creating Schools That Work

Thank you for picking this book up! It is dedicated to establishing the perspective of teacher researchers and the extraordinary ways teachers find solutions to the challenges they face every day. Essentially this is an account of how teachers at one middle school use the frameworks of professional learning communities and action research to guide their professional behaviors.

In reality, however, this book is so much more. There are few texts today devoted to promoting the voice of the teacher in classroom-based research despite the fact that it is those very teachers who must educate children in an increasingly complex educational landscape. The editors trust this book sets the record straight and shows that teachers can and do adapt their practice, seek new strategies, and collaborate to find solutions to the myriad of dilemmas they face each year. This collection of stories stands apart in one more extraordinary respect—they take place within and across a single school site in which the administrators deliberately set out to foster a culture of inquiry.

While this book is written by teachers for teachers, none of the initiatives described in the following chapters would be possible without the visionary leadership of school and district administration. In order for collaborative teacher research to become the norm, this book should be read by teachers, administrators, teacher educators, and staff developers. This book has implications for each of these stakeholder groups, as we *all* seek to improve the quality of the educational process. Welcome!

SOME ASSUMPTIONS ABOUT THIS BOOK

Before going any further, we have some assumptions about the role and the influence of the teacher in P–12 education today. The fundamental premise that underpins this book is that many of the solutions to the problems teachers face on a daily basis are not to be found in new laws passed by the United States Congress and enacted by the federal Department of Education.

Further, the editors believe that most of the solutions will not emanate from state Department of Education mandates or policy changes. In fact, it is even difficult for school-district personnel to maintain constant support for individual schools, let alone individual classrooms. Whatever the good intentions and however meritorious the initiative, these policy makers simply haven't accrued sufficient experience within the complex and unique context of each school.

This book is designed to give a practical set of examples in order to empower skilled educators to see their roles in finding solutions to dilemmas faced in their schools. The concept of empowerment is most often associated with organizational management associated with the building of personal self-esteem and motivation. However, Lichtenstein, McLaughlin, and Knudsen (1991, 5) frame empowerment in the context of education, concluding that empowered teachers possess three essential kinds of knowledge:

- knowledge of professional community,
- knowledge of education policy, and
- knowledge of subject area.

In this text we share the work of teachers who have deliberately constructed professional communities within their school, are cognizant of district and state policies that influence the curriculum they teach and their teaching pedagogies, and who are committed to ongoing professional development as an essential aspect of their professional expertise and competence.

We hope that after reading the teachers' vignettes, you will reconnect with your capacity for professional decision making and see yourself growing as an empowered professional. We recognize that in recent years decision making has become more centralized. This book assumes that in order to maximize the ability of P–12 education to influence the next generation of learners, teachers' professional knowledge should not be marginalized.

Our final assumption involves the importance of your specific school. It may seem trite to simply say every school is different, but this is indeed the case. Your student population is different in some demographic manner from your neighboring school. Perhaps the distinction is related to ethnicity, socio-economics, or home language, but to some degree your school is distinct.

Similarly, the teaching cadre will be different. Perhaps in terms of teaching experience, content expertise, or the number of teachers relative to school population, your teaching faculty is different from every school around you. The inherent administrative philosophy, experience, training, interpersonal skills, vision, and longevity (to name but a few dispositions) will fundamentally shape the school culture as well. In short, your school has its own idiosyncratic culture.

You will undoubtedly have some relative strengths across the school as well as some areas that faculty and administration are both aware need improvement. In summary, this book assumes the solutions to the challenges faced by educators in the United States today will in large part be found at the individual school site, and that these solutions will originate from empowered teachers working within the unique context of their own school.

THE STORY OF SEVEN SPRINGS MIDDLE SCHOOL

Seven Springs Middle School (SSMS) is located in Pasco County, Florida, just north of the Tampa metropolitan area. It is a suburban school of approximately 1,200 sixth through eighth grade students. It faces the same challenges as schools the length and breadth of this country, seeking to advance achievement in an ever more diverse student population, with decreasing resources and increasing accountability measures. In this sense, SSMS could be found in many communities. The District School Board of Pasco County has a history of being regarded statewide as forward-thinking and progressive, and supportive of school administration. With the support of the district, the administration and teachers at SSMS embarked on an innovative journey. This is their story.

Laying the Groundwork

This book is based on the linkages found between two increasingly popular constructs in education today—professional learning communities and action research. We believe they exist together, much like two sides of the same coin. In chapters 2 and 3 of this book these two central tenets are introduced separately, but in reality we recognize they are inextricably bound.

We assert that enterprise resulting from the collaborative interactions of the professional learning community would invariably include ways to research and improve the quality of teaching. On the other side of the coin, research in the school context would be most effective within a structure that supported the collaborative professional development of faculty. Hence, the mutually inclusive relationship between professional learning communities and action research.

The Voices of the Administration and Teachers

In chapter 4 you will meet Chris Christoff and Matt Gruhl, the principal and assistant principal of SSMS during the events described in this book. It is often said that schools reflect the leadership styles of their administrators. Chris and Matt certainly confirmed this, using their own voice to describe their vision, their purpose, and the practical structures they created to facilitate professional learning communities and teacher research in their school. Chapter 4 is a "must read" for all educators interested in how schools plan for collaborative success.

The following six chapters reflect the administrators' efforts. Encouraged, even pushed, to challenge themselves as professional educators, the SSMS teachers describe in their own words how they came to view professional development in a new light. We read how the teachers grappled with and then embraced the new culture of inquiry infused in their school, and describe their action research using the framework laid out in chapter 3.

Their accounts are personal, honest, and practical. Some teachers used the culture of research to push the dynamic of instruction in new directions, others focused on the more immediate pressures associated with student achievement testing, but all of the teachers' stories included in this book are grounded in the classroom. We believe each reader will be able to see her or his own personal entry points into the process of collaborative professional development and research within these stories. We suspect you will see yourselves and your colleagues many times as you read on.

This book concludes with some thoughts on the lessons we should all learn from the Seven Springs Middle School experience. Critical aspects drawn from each chapter are summarized and conclusions about the key conditions for success are explicitly articulated. When you close this book we trust you will have a portrait of how research within the professional community can empower teachers, administrators, and students. Above all, we trust you will agree that you can do this too!

REFERENCES

Darling-Hammond, L. (1997). *The Right to Learn: A Blueprint for Creating Schools That Work*. San Francisco: Jossey-Bass.

Lichtenstein, G., McLaughlin M., & Knudsen, J. (1991). *Teacher Empowerment and Professional Knowledge*. Brunswick, NJ: Consortium for Policy Research and Improvement.

2

Professional Learning Communities

Setting the Stage for Collaboration

Christine Crocco

PLCs are more than just collaborative working arrangements or faculty groups that meet regularly. A PLC is a way of working where staff engage in purposeful, collegial learning. This learning is intentional and its purpose is to improve staff effectiveness so students will be more successful learners.

—Shirley Hord, "What Is a PLC?"

REALIZING THE POTENTIAL OF AN UNTAPPED RESOURCE

When teachers get together outside of work, their spouses and friends are often heard commiserating, "Can they ever talk about anything other than school and their kids?" The fact of the matter is that teachers love to talk about teaching and learning. Traditionally, their workday has not allowed the time for such conversations, and leadership has not recognized the potential for positive change that such conversations could hold.

The issues revealed in these informal contexts have remained largely unresolved due to a lack of infrastructure that would stimulate actions beneficial to students based upon shared professional knowledge. Rosenholtz, McLaughlin and Talbert, and Darling-Hammond began highlighting the importance of working conditions that would create the professional climate for purposeful exchange, such as institutional support for teaching professionals, opportunities for collaborative inquiry, and the process of shared decision making, to the overall success of the organization (Darling-Hammond, 1996; McLaughlin & Talbert, 1993; Rosenholtz, 1989).

This research made the connection between the presence of a strong sense of teachers' self-worth that exists in supportive work environments and the impact on both student achievement and the job satisfaction that retains teachers in the profession. Darling-Hammond noted that although such efforts were at that time "scattered rather than systematic," new structures that would provide time for teachers to reflect and opportunities to share in decision making were becoming more prevalent than ever before (Darling-Hammond, 1996, 9).

THE RISE OF PROFESSIONAL LEARNING COMMUNITIES

The movement to generate a more systemic approach to an infrastructure that would promote teacher collaboration, learning, and inquiry soon began to take shape with the name. When the concept of the professional learning community (PLC) first flashed across the radar screens of educators in the late 1990s, many embraced the idea of working collaboratively to improve their schools. School leaders and teachers attended training that defined the PLC and its characteristics and the kinds of activities in which PLCs might engage. They read and discussed the research about the positive outcomes achieved by schools operating as PLCs. Many schools created teams and called them "PLCs."

PLCs: A Word of Warning

Unfortunately (some might say predictably), after the initial excitement, these teams reverted to business as usual and operated in much the same way as before. Teachers rolled their eyes and groused about reporting for "PLC time." Thus the inevitable realization: acting as a PLC meant more than conducting team or department meetings, more than completing a book study, more than creating leadership teams, and more than the principal espousing the school's mission and vision.

When these in-name-only PLCs failed to yield student achievement results that matched what school leaders and teachers had heard and read about, PLCs began to drift the way of past educational reform efforts. Their potential for changing the way educators work together began to diminish. Andy Hargreaves describes the promise of PLCs as an "an optimistic alternative to educators who hang on to loftier learning goals, and to those who believe that professional reflection and collaboration rather than prescription and compliance are still the best ways to achieve [the outcomes we seek]" (2008, ix).

Hargreaves pointed out that PLCs are vulnerable to the priorities of the prevailing educational policy. He asserted that PLCs could be the impetus to improve and expand students' motivation to learn, and extend and sustain community reflection central to teaching; or they could be hijacked by those focused on high-stakes tests, reinforcing prescriptive compliance around a narrow definition of curriculum.

His urgent tone is clear: "For these reasons, professional learning communities now need more than passionate and practical advocacy. They also need moral discernment and intelligent critique to distinguish the serious from the superficial, the politically opportune from the authentic and profound" (Hargreaves, 2008, x).

Hargreaves recognized that if PLCs are not authentic and grounded in the work of teachers and learners then the value of the community interaction could be lost altogether. As Rick DuFour reminds us, "A school does not become a PLC by enrolling in a program, renaming existing practices, taking the PLC pledge, or learning the secret PLC handshake. A school becomes a professional learning community only when the educators within it align their practices with PLC concepts" (DuFour, 2007, 4). This book is about *situated, purposeful, and collaborative professional behavior* that leads to an *authentic* professional learning community.

How Can PLCs Succeed?

Realizing what is at stake, proponents have refocused on the critical characteristics of the PLC from a more action-oriented perspective. DuFour (2004) warned that professional learning communities had reached a critical juncture and were in danger of suffering the same "this too shall pass" fate that we have seen with other well-intentioned reform efforts. Teachers know that when they talk to other teachers, good things happen for kids. How might educators build on this notion and realize a greater return in terms of visible student progress?

Teachers meeting together is a fine beginning, but conversations and information sharing alone will not lead to improved outcomes for students. The fundamental element that distinguishes the PLC from typical committee or faculty meetings is the intentional, goal-oriented focus on learning. Subgroups of teams without an overarching whole school structure or unified purpose will not move a school toward a common goal (Hord & Sommers, 2008, 145).

DuFour, DuFour, Eaker, and Many (2006) defined the PLC as "educators committed to working collaboratively in ongoing processes of collective inquiry and action research to achieve better results for the students they serve.

Professional learning communities operate under the assumption that the key to improved learning for students is continuous job-embedded learning for educators" (DuFour et al., 2006, 217). This stronger emphasis on action orientation is no accident . . . we know what the right things to do are. We need to *do* them!

LINKING KEY PLC CHARACTERISTICS TO ACTION

Taking meaningful action that yields student results begins with collaborative groups of teachers examining critical questions such as those that DuFour et al. pose for PLCs. They suggest the following:

1) What knowledge and skills should every student acquire as a result of this unit of instruction?
2) How will we know when each student has acquired the essential knowledge and skills?
3) How will we respond when some students do not learn?
4) How will we respond when some students have achieved the intended outcomes? (DuFour et al. 2006, 21)

The answers to these questions, although revealing, must be followed by specific actions in order to transform the ways in which teachers respond to student needs. Without purposeful collaboration dedicated to testing and reflecting on solutions to issues raised by the questions, the conversation generally stops there and leads nowhere.

Thus, the questions for schools striving to operate as PLCs have become: How do we avoid the cycle of reading about, talking about, and otherwise preparing to become a PLC that can seem to last for years? How do school leaders and their faculties operationalize the actions that produce results? How do they build upon those results to create sustainable momentum that will inspire the institutionalization of the PLC?

The purpose of collaboration can only be accomplished if the professionals who are engaged in collective learning are connecting their knowledge to action. It has been our experience that committed educators may come to the table with the best of intentions but lack the facilitative processes and protocols that lead to significant results. When this happens, the unfortunate result is frustration—and a retreat back to the isolation of the status quo. This can be avoided by developing in teachers and school leaders the skills to utilize time efficiently and assess progress toward goals.

While there are many useful online and print resources available to help school and district leaders learn such skills and begin to establish the infrastructure and culture that will nurture professional learning communities, we recommend *Learning by Doing* (DuFour et al., 2006) as one practical resource for those seeking both information about professional learning communities and tools to move forward. The following table summarizes DuFour's review of key characteristics found in PLCs and specific examples of accompanying actions.

This book illustrates what teachers can accomplish when they translate the thoughts and ideas found in table 2.1 into actions, in ways that make a profound difference in their lives and those of their students.

THE ROLE OF LEADERSHIP

If PLCs are to realize their vast potential for transforming schools, strong and informed leadership is vital. The challenge for school and district leaders is setting a vision for and then instituting a culture that produces substantive collaborative interactions among teachers. In many cases, this requires demolishing and rebuilding existing climates and cultures full of entrenched barriers.

If leaders are to maximize the efforts of teachers for the benefit of all students, barriers must be chipped away to open the path to true collaboration. By modeling clarity of focus, protecting time for teachers to collaborate, and offering training so teachers are prepared with protocols and other structures to ensure that collaborative time is efficient and results-oriented, school leaders set the stage for collaboration. Working collaboratively represents a true paradigm shift for many teachers, whether they have spent their careers in "private practice" or enter the profession with the expectation that they will operate in isolation.

A principal's expressed rationale for changing what individual teachers perceive as successful practice must be evidenced by visible support if schools are to evolve from "pockets of excellence" to organizations that own the responsibility for the learning of all students and the professionals who work so hard for positive outcomes. Professional teachers truly do learn by doing and reflecting with colleagues on the results of their work.

Leaders set the tone by continually overseeing and adjusting the necessary conditions for this kind of climate, whether that entails adjusting schedules, equipping teachers with tools and resources, or affording a venue for the public sharing of collaborative work to inform stakeholders.

Table 2.1 The Key Characteristics of the Professional Learning Community

PLC Characteristics	Suggested Actions
1. *Focus on Learning:* The essence of a PLC is a focus on and commitment to the learning of each student.	• Create and commit to a clear vision • Specify results-oriented goals • Clarify what each student must learn • Monitor each student's learning on a timely basis • Provide systematic interventions for struggling learners • Extend and enrich students who have mastered intended learning • Adults continue their own learning through job-embedded practices
2. *Collaborative Culture:* A PLC is composed of teams whose members work interdependently to achieve common goals linked to the purpose of learning for all—students and faculty.	• Work systematically in interdependent teams in order to impact their classroom practice to produce better results for students
3. *Collective Inquiry:* Teams inquire into best practices in teaching and learning and examine the current level of their practice and student achievement. They share knowledge and remain open to new ideas as they develop new skills. Eventually, this will shift beliefs and attitudes that transform the school culture.	• Engage in inquiry into best practices for teaching and learning • Build shared knowledge • Develop new skills through the inquiry process
4. *Action Orientation:* PLC members are action-oriented and learn by doing. They turn aspirations into actions and visions into reality.	• Findings from inquiry are shared and put into action • Results of the action are studied

5. *Continuous Improvement:* PLCs are characterized by a persistent disquiet with the status quo and a constant search for better ways to achieve goals and fulfill the organization's purpose.	• Engage in ongoing cycles to search for better ways of achieving goals:
	  ○ Gather evidence of current reality
	  ○ Develop strategies to build on strengths and address weaknesses
	  ○ Implement strategies
	  ○ Analyze the impact of the strategies to determine what was effective and what was not
	  ○ Apply the new knowledge in the next cycle
	• Use these cycles to create an atmosphere of perpetual learning that is a way of doing business

Table 2.1   The Key Characteristics of the Professional Learning Community

PLC Characteristics	Suggested Actions
6. Results Orientation: Members of a PLC realize that their efforts must be assessed on the basis of the results they achieve rather than their intentions.	• Each team develops and pursues measurable goals aligned with school and district goals • Teams create common formative assessments to gather evidence of learning • Teams review the results to identify and address programmatic areas of concern • Teams review results to discover individual strengths and weaknesses in their teaching in order to learn from one another • Teams use the assessments to identify students who need additional time and support for their learning

Adapted from DuFour et al. (2006), 3–5.

It is no easy task to build the trust necessary for such an environment. Teachers as learners need to begin where they are and receive the encouragement from their leaders and colleagues to experience the practices of high functioning PLCs. As trust builds, the confidence to take risks grows proportionately. Figure 2.1 illustrates Crocco, Wiggins, and McClamma's (2004) model of how teachers might move along a continuum of possible PLC actions that yield higher impact on student achievement as they take greater risks to de-privatize their practices. The ultimate goal is to develop an honest and truly collaborative culture that benefits students—and teachers!

We can also draw inspiration from those on the path of this journey. An excellent resource for leaders fostering PLCs is *Leading Professional Learning Communities: Voices from Research and Practice*, by Hord and Sommers (2008). Their examination of components of the PLC, leadership strategies, policies, and behaviors serve as a practical guide for those who are building a culture of collaboration in their schools.

ACTION RESEARCH IN THE PLC

Those who recognize the power of the PLC are utilizing action research as one vehicle to energize collaborative teams. Cycles of action research allow teachers to respond directly to the issues that confront them every day. Mike Schmoker sees these short cycles as the catalyst for the "tipping point" that

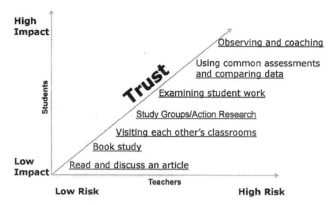

Figure 2.1   The Relationship between Teacher Behaviors and Student Achievement

will combine thought and action, producing the change that "spreads like a contagion" (Schmoker, 2004, 430).

Schmoker recognizes what Valerie Janesick describes as the elastic quality (Janesick, 2000) of such work: "Actual practice must adjust and respond to ground-level complexities that can't be precisely anticipated at the beginning of the year; it must adapt to the results of specific strategies that cannot be conceived in advance" (Schmoker, 2004, 425). Continuous cycles of action research provide a framework for educators to explore the "messy work" of teaching, search for answers to pedagogical questions, reflect on findings, and celebrate successes along the way.

The Inquiry-Oriented PLC

The chapters of our book illustrate a promising path toward what Nancy Fichtman Dana and Diane Yendol-Hoppey describe as inquiry-oriented PLCs (2008). They introduce this as a new entity, linking together the two concepts of PLC and action research in a way that greatly enhances professional knowledge and growth. Their books, *The Reflective Educator's Guide to Professional Development* (2008) and *The Reflective Educator's Guide to Classroom Research* (2009), will help you explore the nuances of combining these two concepts in order to achieve what the authors call the "ultimate goal . . . to create an inquiry stance toward teaching" (Dana and Yendol-Hoppey, 2009, 7).

As teachers research the questions they wonder about, they can apply their findings in the context of their classrooms to help students right away. The point here is that action research doesn't occur in a vacuum. As school leaders develop the key characteristics of PLCs, they nurture the climate in which the investigative wonderings of teachers flourish. PLCs and action research have much in common, and the idea of linking the two together as Fichtman Dana and Yendol-Hoppey have done is much more rewarding than continuing to have them travel down parallel paths.

We strive to build on their work and that of others such as Linda Darling-Hammond, who connected these concepts in her book *The Right to Learn* (1997), in which she made the case for the importance of teaching for understanding and the complex set of skills needed for this to occur. "Learning to practice in substantially different ways than one has ever before experienced can occur neither through theoretical imaginings alone nor through unguided experience alone. Instead it requires a tight coupling of the two" (Darling-Hammond, 1997).

We assert that action research can become a natural and seamless part of professional development when it is nested in a broader school culture that respects and encourages teacher communication and community. Teachers must be empowered and given permission to take risks and practice a philosophy of deliberative and positive change. Teachers make the difference. There is no simpler or more powerful statement.

The teachers who wrote from their hearts for this book are dedicated to their students and their colleagues and honest about their triumphs and their challenges. We hope that you find personal relevance to your own practice as you read their powerful stories about growing professionally and delivering high quality instruction to *all* children.

Our children are counting on those educators closest to them. They are counting on you and your colleagues working collectively for them. Together we can gain the attention and support of national, state, and local policy makers to fully empower professional educators to do their best work on behalf of students.

REFERENCES

Crocco, C. M., Wiggins, L., & McClamma, B. (2004). *Teacher Leaders at Work: Facilitating Study Groups.* Presentation for the Pasco County Staff Development Office, Land O' Lakes, FL.

Dana, N. F., & Yendol-Hoppey, D. (2009). *The Reflective Educator's Guide to Classroom Research, Second Edition.* Thousand Oaks, CA: Corwin Press.

———. (2008). *The Reflective Educator's Guide to Professional Development.* Thousand Oaks, CA: Corwin Press.

Darling-Hammond, L. (March 1996). The Quiet Revolution: Rethinking Teacher Development. *Educational Leadership* 53(6): 4–10.

———. (1997). *The Right to Learn.* San Francisco, CA: Jossey-Bass, Inc.

DuFour, R. (May 2004). What Is a Professional Learning Community? *Educational Leadership* 61(8): 6–11.

———. (September 2007). Professional Learning Communities: A Bandwagon, an Idea Worth Considering, or Our Best Hope for High Levels of Learning? *Middle School Journal* 39(1): 4–8.

DuFour, R., Dufour, R., Eaker, R., & Many, T. (2006). *Learning by Doing: A Handbook for Professional Learning Communities at Work.* Bloomington, IN: Solution Tree.

Hargreaves, A. (2008). In Hord & Sommers, *Leading Professional Learning Communities: Voices from Research and Practice.* Thousand Oaks, CA: Corwin Press.

Hord, S. M. (2007). What is a PLC? Southwest Educational Development Laboratory Letter, XIX (I). Retrieved from http://www.sedl.org/pubs/magazine/archive.html.

Hord, S. M., & Sommers, W. A. (2008). *Leading Professional Learning Communities: Voices from Research and Practice.* Thousand Oaks, CA: Corwin Press.

Janesick, V. (2000). The Choreography of Qualitative Research Design: Minuets, Improvisation, and Crystallization. In N. Denzin & Y. Lincoln, (Eds.), *Handbook of Qualitative Research* (379–99). Thousand Oaks, CA: Sage.

McLaughlin, M. W., & Talbert, J. E. (1993). *Contexts That Matter for Teaching and Learning.* Stanford, CA: Center for Research on the Context of Secondary School Teaching, Stanford University.

Rosenholtz, S. (1989). *Teacher's workplace: The social organization of schools.* New York: Longman.

Schmoker, M. (February 2004). Tipping Point: From Feckless Reform to Substantive Instructional Improvement. *Phi Delta Kappan* 85(6): 424–432.

3

Demystifying Action Research

A Practical Explanation for Teacher Researchers

Roger Brindley

> With respect to research, teachers have traditionally been seen primarily as subjects or consumers of research done by others. The difference with teacher research is that it is not research on other people, nor is it developed around topics deemed important by other people. Rather, teacher research involves teachers directly in the selection of immediate, compelling, and meaningful topics to explore with respect to their own practice.
>
> Furthermore it is teachers themselves who carry out the research on their own work in order to improve what they do, including how they work with and for others. In these respects teacher research treats teachers as autonomous, responsible agents who participate actively in directing their own work and their own professional development.
>
> —Ken Zeichner and Mary Klehr, *Teacher Research as Professional Development for P–12 Educators*

In this chapter we endeavor to demystify action research. We begin by establishing three recommended models for action research but then quickly turn to describing this thing we call "action research" within the school context. We take a step-by-step approach to describing the research process and use a set of examples that we hope will help teacher researchers to imagine placing action research within their professional work.

FINDING AN APPROACH THAT WORKS FOR YOU

There are a number of researchers who recommend various steps in the action research process. Most are very similar and while they vary in the

Table 3.1 Three Models for Action Research

Emily Calhoun	Ernie Stringer	Robert Bullough and Andrew Gitlin
Phase 1: Selecting an area or focus	*Step 1*: Design the study	*Phase 1*: A concern or issue is identified and written up
Phase 2: Collecting data	*Step 2*: Gather the data	*Phase 2*: Write a plan for addressing the concern, implement and gather data
Phase 3: Organizing data		
Phase 4: Analyzing and inter-preting data	*Step 3*: Analyze the data	*Phase 3*: Review the data to determine the effect of the plan
Phase 5: Taking action	*Step 4*: Use the outcomes	

number of stages and language used they are closely related conceptually. Three of the well-regarded models come from Emily Calhoun (1994), Robert Bullough and Andrew Gitlin (1995), and Ernie Stringer (2004). Table 3.1 summarizes the stages in their models.

All the researchers start by identifying the phenomenon to be studied and, through a process of collecting and analyzing data, arrive at a data-driven rationale for change. They advocate for a varying number of phases but essentially these three models are complementary. It is our experience that sometimes teachers perceive this process to be too technical or complex and language such as "data" evokes unsettling images of white lab coats, clipboards, and experiments. In the following section we will demystify the action research process.

We will provide you with common language to describe a simple process that has enormous potential to improve outcomes at your school. We will do this by using a hybrid approach to the models in table 3.1. For each stage of the process we will share a hypothetical example. Our intent is to present action research as an authentic, meaningful, effective, and manageable approach to seeking solutions to the very real dilemmas teachers and administrators face in the elementary, middle, and high school every week of the year.

GETTING STARTED

The first stage in action research is discussing what concerns you. One day spent as a fly on the wall in your teachers' lounge will probably reveal some of the concerns across the teaching faculty. Another day shadowing a principal will give some important perspective. Fundamentally, educators need to ask themselves, "What are the issues in my classroom or my grade or my content area that I would like to find answers for? What are the schoolwide needs that we should be addressing?" Then start asking your school administration and/or other teachers what they think.

You'll need to empower yourself. Be sure to be strategic in whom you ask. We all work with colleagues who see the glass as half-full and others who view it as half-empty. If you ask a colleague known as a skeptic or a cynic, you'll likely get a response that inhibits your desire to see positive change. So who are the colleagues you enjoy working with? Who are the free thinkers and the brainstormers? Start by asking them.

Working on an Individual Goal

Some of these conversations may simply be an opportunity to explore ideas and to see if there is a "goodness of fit" between your personal vision for improvement and those of other colleagues. Indeed, it may be that your concerns are clearly individual to you. There may be some pressing issue in your specific classroom that you seek a solution for and that, through discussion with colleagues, you gain advice and ideas to help you.

This kind of informal mentorship of each other and stewardship of our profession is vital. It might be that just one colleague agrees to assist you. Perhaps it's a department chair who can observe your room or a teaching friend who agrees to meet on a consistent basis with you as you work through the dilemma and the possible solutions.

Be sure that you have a clear goal and know what you want to accomplish. Understand that this kind of preemptive, purposeful examination of your practice is vital to your professional growth and to the trust you feel for your colleagues. Trying to find solutions with the help of an "expert other" is essential to influencing student achievement. So your action research may be yours alone and your research support may involve the trusted insights of a valued colleague or colleagues.

Working Together

Other conversations will lead to some common ideas that become the repeated focus of your discussions. Given the structures found in schools, it may be that this group of colleagues already shares ideas frequently. It may

Box 3.1   The Hypothetical
Example—Parents' Involvement in the PTA

Encouraging parent involvement in the Parent Teacher Association is a common concern. It seems that many schools from small rural elementary schools to large urban high schools have to be creative when addressing this issue. For that reason, it's a simple but authentic example. It probably wouldn't take many school educators long to agree that at their school they have room for improvement in encouraging parent communication and involvement. For this example we will focus on PTA participation. So, as we get started, the question to be answered is, "How do we get more parents involved in the PTA?"

be a grade-level team, department colleagues, planning teams, or a representative school committee.

As you continue your discussions common concerns may emerge. You may agree as a group that there are common issues you face together and together you may wonder how to address these mutual problems. Perhaps a thoughtful administrator shares a broader perspective on patterns or trends he or she sees developing across a content area or grade level. Comments such as, "I wish there was a way to . . ." and "What if we were to . . ." will begin to arise. Be sure to establish what the concern is, and what the question is that you want to find answers for. As a group have a clear idea of what you would like to accomplish. Be realistic. The first steps are usually small steps.

COLLECTING YOUR DATA

Depending on your wonderings and the question(s) that you have, the kinds of information you need to collect will vary. The key here is to find the information that answers your question. Whom do you need to talk to? What information are you hoping that person will be able to share? How can you get to the heart of your question and collect information that informs you?

Involving the School Community

If you need to connect with individual people, you might want to shadow that person or meet with them one-on-one to ask them direct questions, essentially as an interviewer. If you really want to get the thoughts of several people with relevant experiences to your question, you could meet with them individually; but if you believe that these members of the school community can share with each other (such as a school committee, a grade-level teaching team, a high school department, or business partners), you could interview them together as a focus group.

You will need to judge whether your questions would encourage them to speak freely and whether the relationships of these stakeholders allow for you to bring them all together. Sometimes if opinions are contentious, focus groups can be problematic, so we recommend you ask a colleague who has experience with conducting focus groups to help you. At other times the participants feed off each other's ideas and share extensions they wouldn't have thought of otherwise. The subsequent synthesis of ideas generates more helpful comments. The sum can be greater than the parts!

Then again, you might need to ask a much larger group of people. Perhaps you want the thoughts of every teacher in your school or every parent of a student in fifth grade. At this point you probably need to generate a questionnaire or survey. Consider carefully what you want to ask, how long you would like the survey to take to answer, how quickly you want it returned, and so forth.

Sometimes questions call for you to collect materials as well as, or instead of, talking to people. For example, to understand how differentiated instruction is successfully delivered in a classroom you probably need to observe and take your own notes. You might need to keep your own teacher's log or diary, or ask those who can answer your questions best to do so. Perhaps you need to be collecting examples of students' work, colleagues' planning materials, or curricular texts.

Resources to Guide You

At this point you might be thinking, "What have I gotten myself into?" The intent of this book is to share some illustrative and practical examples of teachers who have been able to enrich their professional work and the power of the school in the community through action research.

While working collaboratively and building a climate of shared knowledge and inquiry will help us to be better teachers and our students to be more successful, we do recognize that if you are starting out this can be daunting. You will need the support of your colleagues and administration. Fortunately, there are many "how-to" action research books available. Simply go to your favorite online bookseller and search for "action research." The choices are numerous but four excellent paperback examples are:

Dana, Nancy F., & Yendol-Hoppey, Diane. (2009). *The Reflective Educator's Guide to Classroom Research, Second Edition*. Thousand Oaks, CA: Corwin Press.

Mills, Geoffrey. (2007). *Action Research: A Guide for the Teacher Researcher*. Upper Saddle River, NJ: Pearson.

Sagor, Richard. (2000). *Guiding School Improvement with Action Research*. Alexandria, VA: Association for Supervision and Curriculum Development

Stringer, Ernie. (2004). *Action Research in Education*. Upper Saddle River, NJ: Pearson.

As the information you are collecting begins to accumulate, be sure to keep it organized and in a safe place. As a rule, unless you are engaging your students in the research process (particularly in the secondary school), consider keeping the paperwork with your personal files. Password-protected downloaded and scanned files are an excellent idea too.

ORGANIZING AND MAKING SENSE OF YOUR DATA

Analysis is another of those words that conjures up images of rooms full of computers whirring away, statistical formulas, and mathematical computations. So we will use the phrase "making sense" instead of "analysis" because that is in reality an accurate description of this work. Sorting through all the information you have collected can be time-consuming. Unless you are trying to shed some light on a specific question relevant to the idiosyn-

Box 3.2   The Hypothetical
Example—Parents' Involvement in the PTA

In our example your action research group agrees to develop a needs assessment on behalf of the PTA and then sends the survey home to all the parents in the school to find out when, where, and under what conditions they would be more willing to become involved. The survey asks parents what stumbling blocks inhibit their participation and their suggestions for increasing parent involvement in the PTA. Then you bring the entire PTA board together as a focus group. Finally interviews gather the thoughts of the school administration and selected students, so that the research group has several different perspectives. You can see this set of data would grow quickly.

crasies of your own classroom and really need to work alone so you have a thorough understanding of all aspects of the issue, we recommend making sense of the information collected collaboratively.

Another Pair of Eyes!

Working as a group allows you to pool your thoughts. It allows you to confirm that others have the same understanding you do. It allows you to brainstorm aloud and theorize about what the data is telling you. Best of all another pair of eyes, or several pairs of eyes, might catch something in the information that you missed and allows you to combine your thinking about the most important ideas in the information. You certainly can do this work alone, but you can often reveal more about your data when working collaboratively, and besides it can be fun!

Again, there are many action research texts to help guide you on the process of analysis. For our purposes we want to simply capture the foundational process. Start by numbering every page. Later in this process as you talk with your colleagues you will be able to immediately refer to a particular page number.

Then it's time to read! We recommend that as you read the data, be it a survey, a student response, or the comments made in an interview, you should familiarize yourself with the information. Try to pull out the big ideas from the information. What are the key meanings in the data? What was this person or this group trying to tell you? Make a list of these big ideas or meanings for each piece of data. Then move on to the next piece of data.

Letting the Big Ideas Bubble Up!

One of the gratifying aspects of asking questions is that you often get similar answers or comments that are related to each other—not always, but often. As you continue to read through the information and list the big ideas for each piece of data some common notions will begin to develop. You might see some patterns in the responses or several people who have common ideas. If you then start to list these similar thoughts together as a group, you will be categorizing the information. Researchers sometimes describe this process as "letting the data speak to you" and these categories as "emergent themes."

The more data you read the more some themes will develop. Other themes might need to be combined together because you realize they are very similar. Be flexible. The first pieces of data you look at may, or may not, be representative of the whole set of information, but you won't know that until your have read all the data. So it's okay if some emerging themes get combined or collapsed together.

Making sense of data is a little bit like trying to fly a plane as you build it! You won't know precisely what conclusions you can draw until the analysis is well advanced. This is part of the value of working collaboratively, so that you have colleagues who are also very familiar with the information that you can share your ideas with.

As the process of making sense continues, you might have a few written or spoken comments that are illustrative of an emerging theme. Make a note of where those comments are in your data so you can access them quickly later when it comes time to share your results. Be sure to discuss what label you want to give each emerging theme. You'll enjoy brainstorming a myriad of different titles you could give a group of data. Try to find a title that captures the essence of that theme.

A Couple of Ideas to Help You Think through Your Data

There are two more recommendations we would like to make. First, we suggested that most answers will fall into common groups or themes, but the responses that don't fit neatly into any particular theme are very important. These "outlying" responses might represent the thoughts of a cultural minority in your school such as first-language Spanish students, students who are vegetarians, Seventh-Day Adventists, extended family members who are guardians, and so on.

This list is virtually endless, but we do not want to somehow relegate or ignore these comments, or appear to be doing so despite our best efforts to the contrary. These comments may be infrequent and unable to fit into one of your developing themes, but note them and report them nonetheless. Each piece of data should be weighed equally.

Secondly, another resource to assist you with this work will be your local universities. If you have a relationship with the school or college of education, use your connections to locate the teacher educators vested in school-based research. Perhaps a course instructor can suggest some names. Alternatively, an intern supervisor who visits your school might have a great suggestion on whom to contact. Collegial university faculty vested in bridging theory and practice, or known for research that involves school teachers, can be wonderful "friends." They often have experience collecting and analyzing data and then writing up the results.

Box 3.3   The Hypothetical
Example—Parents' Involvement in the PTA

Now that we have collected the surveys from the parents, we can begin to read their perceptions of the PTA. The themes that emerge include the ideas that (1) some parents don't see the point and report the PTA as not relevant to them; (2) PTA meeting times are inconvenient on weekday evenings when children have to be fed, homework has to be completed, and basketball practice takes priority; (3) some parents have access problems, such as one-car families needing their vehicle elsewhere or the lack of reliable public transportation in the evening; and (4) many parents indicate a communication problem, claiming that the PTA announcements are buried in the school website and that their children do not get the PTA meeting announcement sheets home to them. So results indicate four themes: "PTA lacks relevancy," "Transportation is difficult," "Evenings are packed," and "PTA communication."

Frequently, the university has an expectation they will be involved in research and allots them time to complete research. This means that not only do they expect to write as part of their professional behavior but they have nurtured their own writing skills. Most importantly, most university faculty working in schools want to develop partnerships. They understand that research is a collaborative team effort, and they want to honor the perspectives and "voices" of their school-based colleagues. So be brave! Reach out and find this resource. It is our experience that many of these initial contacts grow into partnerships that last many years.

Through this process you will "make sense" of the data in a very authentic manner. You'll be able to explain what your research group found, give examples, and discuss what conclusions you made. That brings us to the final step in the action research process.

SHARING RESULTS AND TAKING ACTION

The final step to action research is absolutely essential. What good is the time and energy you have invested in addressing an important action research question—that may well affect how many of *your* colleagues and other educators beyond your school would think about *their* work—if you keep that information to yourself? Once your research group has drawn some conclusions from your work, ask yourself two questions. The first is "Who needs to know this?" The second is "How will we act on this information?"

Who Needs to Know?

The short answer is that it depends on your focus. A study of inefficiencies in the school lunchroom should be shared with administration, the cooks, lunchroom assistants, and probably teachers and students. A new reading strategy in third grade might be helpful to all teachers of emerging readers across several grade levels and the school administration, and certainly might be of interest to a district curriculum specialist. The effectiveness of a retention strategy in high school may go to administration, school psychologists, counselors, resource officers, teachers, and possibly parents.

All three of these examples may be helpful in the wider community. It may be prudent to share with some element of the local media, with the staff development experts in the school district, with colleagues at your local university, and at a conference of district, state, regional, or national organizations. Fundamentally, if it's relevant to someone, don't be afraid to share with that person.

Now, you'll want to seek some advice here. For example, your school or district administration may wish you to remove real names or use pseudonyms so as to protect students, colleagues, and the district. Your administration will probably want to read and advise you on any information that goes home to parents. So it is critical to create a plan for sharing and then communicate your plans for disseminating your important information with the appropriate administration so that they are involved and can support you.

Please remember one of the fundamental premises of school-based research. It is the notion that many of the solutions to challenges faced in education today can be found in our local pre-, elementary, middle, and high schools. *How* you share your findings should be carefully discussed, but *whether* you should share your findings should not be up for debate. If you believe your findings are important, you must share them! Isn't that the point?

Acting on This Information

Once you have decided who needs to know, you have to decide on the actions to be taken. There are the actions you will want to take in your own classrooms as teacher researchers and then there is the act of dissemination itself. You will want to decide how to present your work.

While feedback is a constant benefit of sharing, and you should invite your audience to comment, sometimes researchers have already considered their study, made improvements, or instigated new initiatives and want to share that information as well. Alternatively, the data might have left researchers unsure of how to proceed and needing to describe their studies with other educators so they can mutually consider possible solutions.

We will return to this idea later in the chapter. Suffice it to say, it's most appropriate to share that you have improved your understandings and practices and, depending on your study, that you may have identified one possible answer or an area for further investigation. Do not feel that you must have "the answer," as if *one* existed, in order to share.

In your own classrooms your findings will likely cause you to rethink some aspect of your teaching behavior. Perhaps you have a clearer sense of a particular teaching strategy you want to use more, or maybe you now have a fresh or different perspective on an area of content or on the needs of particular students. Maybe your research has led you to reconsider how you deliver the curriculum and your instructional planning.

Sharing with Others

There are also the actions beyond your classroom. Once you have a plan for disseminating, you'll need to present your area of action research. Depending on which educational stakeholders you have identified, you may ask to share in grade level or content area planning, present at a schoolwide faculty meeting, share a written narrative with a school committee or the local school district, create a multimedia presentation for a state conference, invite the local media to visit your school, or write a manuscript for publication in a practitioner or research journal.

This is just a partial list, and you may find yourself experiencing several of these options among others. Use your resources wisely. Administrators can support your work by tacitly endorsing the results of your research with teaching colleagues, by creating time for professional development, or by covering a substitute teacher or some modest travel costs. University colleagues are often accustomed to writing and can be critical friends advising and editing for you or even leading the writing process.

Box 3.4   The Hypothetical
Example—Parents' Involvement in the PTA

Armed with the findings of the PTA action research, a committee instigated some changes. To assist with parent concerns about relevancy, a PTA parent subcommittee for planning meetings is formed. In addition, it is agreed that every PTA meeting should include a showcase event and be more interactive (for example, highlighting a local business supporting the school, parents involved in a fund-raising scheme, a question-and-answer session on the School Improvement Plans or strategic goals, etc.). It is decided that each meeting will also feature students in the school presenting a curricular project, some performing arts, or student initiative.

To address concerns with transportation, the school administration negotiates scheduling the PTA meetings at the local community center directly on a bus route and more centrally located in the district. PTA meeting times are now posted in a dedicated banner space on the home page of the school website, a large weatherproof PTA banner announcing meetings was posted in the car pick-up lane, and parents now sign in at meetings so that the class with the most parent involvement receives a pizza party.

Extending Your Ideas

Lastly, we would suggest that you keep a notepad or diary and monitor how the dissemination process develops. In your own classrooms you'll want to keep your personal thoughts on how your understandings and actions have changed as a part of your reflection-in-action. Beyond your classroom, other teachers in your school might have a great idea or a thoughtful question that you will want to write down. An administrator might have a terrific suggestion for extending your ideas. At a conference, other participants might offer you their relevant experiences and want to exchange e-mail addresses.

Whatever the scenario, do keep a written account of your thoughts and others' ideas. Many of these notes will help you think further about your work as a teacher researcher and as an educational leader.

SOME FINAL THOUGHTS ON ACTION RESEARCH

It is almost inevitable that your research will lead to further questions, and as such the act of presenting your findings will reflect a dynamic, ever-changing, living experience. Contrary to common notions that research helps

THINK

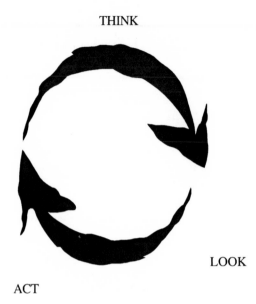

LOOK

ACT

to find "the answer" to a concern, educators understand that the human con-
dition is constantly altering, and that the art and science of teaching is per-
petually evolving. Your experience will probably reflect this, and you will
have gained some insights and possibly answered your original question(s)
but now might be hesitant on how to proceed.

You may have a whole new set of questions as a result of your action
research. Please don't worry! If you have ever heard someone say, "The
day you think you have all the answers you should retire!" you will understand that our chosen career path involves the never-ending journey
of trying to improve our understanding of our world. Ours is a journey
of continuous improvement and lifelong learning. Just like teaching in
general, action research is open-ended and cyclical in nature. It is another
tool for teachers to use as we seek to become better educators and leaders
in our field and in our communities. Put simply, continuous improvement
leads to new questions.

As teachers we must be able to think carefully about our world, to reflect
on and critique our experiences. We must look for patterns, seek solutions,
and problem-solve in order to address a myriad of challenges and opportunities. We have to watch and diligently look, hear what is said and listen
carefully, and then analyze our observations and decide on an action and a
path forward. The endearing quality of action research is that it is a natural
extension of the complex work we would aspire to in any case.

In this book you will read the action research voices of teachers at one middle school, written in their own words. Their candid accounts are illustrative and revealing. Each of these teachers felt empowered by the action research model, and we fervently hope that you too will feel empowered to move forward finding solutions critical to the success of your own school cultures and responsive to the needs of your community.

REFERENCES

Bullough, R., & Gitlin, A. (1995). *Becoming a Student of Teaching: Methodologies for Exploring Self and School Context*. New York: Garland Publishing.

Calhoun, E. (1994). *How to Use Action Research in the Self-renewing School*. Alexandria, VA: Association for Supervision and Curriculum Development.

Dana, N. F., & Yendol-Hoppey, D. (2009). *The Reflective Educator's Guide to Classroom Research, Second Edition*. Thousand Oaks, CA: Corwin Press.

Mills, G. (2007). *Action Research: A Guide for the Teacher Researcher*. Upper Saddle River, NJ: Pearson.

Sagor, R. (2000). *Guiding School Improvement with Action Research*. Alexandria, VA: Association for Supervision and Curriculum Development.

Stringer, E. (2004). *Action Research in Education*. Upper Saddle River, NJ: Pearson.

Zeichner, K., & Klehr, M. (1999). *Teacher Research as Professional Development for P–12 Educators*. Washington, DC: Office of Educational Research and Improvement.

II

CREATING A CULTURE OF INQUIRY

4

The Perspectives of a School Administration

Chris Christoff and Matt Gruhl

*In this chapter a middle school principal and assistant principal
describe in their own words the structures and strategies they built
that allowed for the development of a culture in their school that
fostered action research.*

A MEANS TO AN END: LOOKING BACK
ON PROFESSIONAL DEVELOPMENT AS COMPLIANCE

Imagine working in a new public middle school in a suburban county of
a southern state in 1996. Of the 1,250 sixth through eighth graders being
served at this school, approximately 35 percent received free and reduced
lunch, 25 percent carried the label of being in exceptional student education
(special education), and 15 percent were minorities. The staff included a
mix of competent veteran and new teachers, led by a skilled and charismatic
principal who inspired the faculty. In many ways this school operated in a
manner that reflected that time period.

The Role of Regional Accreditation in Preserving the Status Quo

The principal was an expert in successfully navigating a school through
the Southern Association of Schools (SACS) accreditation process. She
developed a comprehensive plan, where teams of teachers performed tasks
and documented them in order to be compliant. This resulted in a group of
task-oriented teachers that efficiently satisfied accreditation requirements.

Unfortunately, this accreditation process demanded conformity and did not encourage the faculty to reflect further on their practice or instruction. Although isolated pieces of a professional learning community existed, the school put a higher priority on documentation, rather than on professional learning to improve achievement. Does this sound familiar? This was the predicament of Seven Springs Middle School.

The first task to be documented for SACS was the Continuous Improvement Plan (CIP). Once again, the process developed by the principal was very efficient and probably fairly common for that time. Near the end of each school year, an e-mail was sent out by the principal asking for volunteers to write the next year's CIP. The few faculty members that volunteered would meet after school with the principal and share their ideas and perceptions. She genuinely listened and included their thoughts in formulating the CIP. Within four weeks the entire process was complete and the focus for the next year was established.

Since the CIP was developed prior to the release of any summative assessment data, it was based on a series of disconnected teacher perceptions of what students needed. Although teacher perceptions were often very useful in discussing how to improve achievement, in this case, the consideration of actual achievement was partial at best. As a result, a narrow, subjective, and somewhat misguided CIP was developed.

Continuous Improvement: Setting Goals on Paper Only!

The potential weakness of the CIP magnified with implementation. At the beginning of the following year, all teachers received a copy of this plan in their mailboxes, with the expectation that their own Professional Development Plans (PDP) would mirror one of the goals contained in the CIP.

There was no explanation of why the goals were written, nor an explicit explanation that the staff at large would play a part in implementing the outlined strategies. Within the first month of school, each teacher would conference with an administrator to review their PDP based on a CIP goal in which they had no vested interest. This superficial process of planning and goal setting created an environment of compliance and task completion rather than empowerment and ownership.

Secondly, SACS required the documentation of full faculty participation in committees. These committees were chaired by members of the school leadership team, such as department chairs. Not surprisingly, they modeled their committees after the biweekly leadership and monthly staff meetings.

During these meetings, the teachers generally listened to the concerns and information provided by the administration. It was the "sit-and-get mode" that many teachers became comfortable with. Research and problem solving were minimal, and the focus was linear. As a result, committee work became a job requirement rather than a vehicle for change.

Documenting professional development was another essential part of accreditation. At the first staff meeting of each school year, a faculty member was designated to coordinate the staff development efforts throughout the year. This person posted district staff development offerings, calculated and reported in-service points, and determined trainings to be offered on the two designated professional development days.

Similar to the CIP process, the trainings offered at the school were a collection of random ideas generated by the staff development committee. There was no direct connection to the CIP or individual PDPs. This resulted in faculty members developing areas that had no connection to their professional growth or to the academic progress of the students in the school.

After reading the description of Seven Springs Middle School in 1996, it would be easy to believe that the school and its leader were not acting as a professional learning community. True and systemic collaboration seemed rare. Although in one sense this is true, the school operated in the context of an educational era where this was the norm. In comparison to other schools, Seven Springs functioned well given the accountability requirements of the time. Under a savvy principal, who had worked hard to attract good teachers and trusted their actions, Seven Springs Middle School was primed to take the next step toward becoming a professional learning community.

FINDING A SPARK TO IGNITE A FIRE—CHANGING OUR WAYS

In 2004 the original principal retired and one of the existing assistant principals assumed the lead position. Educational policy had recast the role of the principal from functioning as a manager to one focused on instructional leadership. Since the new principal understood the structures of the school, it became very apparent that there was no system in place for sharing, communicating, and empowering, and there was a definite need to move the faculty from a passive to an active stance. Understanding the readiness level of each faculty member was crucial to establishing this change process.

Encouraging an active faculty required a new perspective, so the principal hired an assistant principal from outside of the district who was known for his instructional focus. This is where our story, the account of a principal and assistant principal who held a common vision and high hopes for positive change, began. We just were not sure how it was going to happen!

Learning from the Research

Together we wanted to nurture the growth of a professional learning community where empowered faculty members collaborated to improve student achievement and to generate possible solutions to real, school-based issues. As an administration it was our goal to create the conditions and structures for this type of empowered community to thrive.

Our understanding of empowerment is aligned with Spreitzer and Quinn (2001), who emphasized the importance of self-determination, meaning, competence, impact, guidance, and control in their book, *A Company of Leaders*. "Self-determination" is defined as the freedom of an educator to determine his or her own actions. "Meaning" refers to the notion that teaching is more than a job and that teachers find their work important and may even describe it as a calling. However, to experience meaning teachers must be "competent" and be equipped with the skills and tools to accomplish goals. The loss of competence may result in the loss of meaning.

Spreitzer and Quinn suggest "impact" is best described as the feeling of making a difference and is a vital component of empowerment. Achieving these dimensions involves:

- Developing a catalyst or structure for change,
- Piloting that structure using a common language that leads to a shared understanding of the concepts and goals,
- Soliciting relevant professional partnerships, and
- Providing necessary professional development support.

All of these steps need to be realized in a balanced culture based on trust, support, and guidance.

Setting the Stage

Through our own personal research and district-level professional development, we identified action research groups as a possible vehicle for precipitating change and transforming our isolated and top-down school into a professional learning community of empowered educators. We realized that before implementing a system of action research, we needed to first build capacity.

One simple but critical step in the capacity-building process was to change the way we facilitated faculty meetings. We encouraged our team leaders to take an active role in these meetings by allotting time for best-practice sharing. We also implemented grade level meetings where different teams at the same grade level would share a focus area they were working on to improve teaching and learning.

Another initial step established a common language focused on teaching and learning that we used in our meetings to explicitly define terms that were crucial to a learning community. Terms such as "formative assessment," "active learner," and "research" were defined by analyzing articles in groups and discussing the implications within the context of our school. By modeling how meetings were to be run, we formed an expectation.

All committees at the school were now expected to behave as a learning community, where sharing was not a rare occurrence, but the norm. With changes happening throughout the school, we could tell it was time to start experimenting with a formalized group engaging in action research.

EXPERIMENTING WITH ACTION RESEARCH—THE GUINEA PIG

We knew from the beginning that sustained change had to be teacher-driven and -supported, so we targeted a specific group of faculty members and asked them if they would be interested in piloting the process of action research. We chose the Safety Committee because they played a significant role in a school with over two thousand students and twenty portables in addition to our main building. This group also represented a good cross-section of our faculty, including three basic education teachers, an exceptional student education teacher, a teacher's aide, the School Resource Officer (SRO), and an assistant principal.

With the assistance of a district professional development specialist, we introduced the basic processes of action research to the group. This included the idea of an issue/problem, researching and finding possible solutions to the problem, implementing solutions, and measuring the success both formatively and summatively. One teacher immediately said, "I like this because we can actually do something instead of listening to people talking about nothing at boring, useless meetings." We tried not to take that personally as administrators, but sometimes the truth hurts! It was time to experiment with the process of letting others give instead of having them sit and get.

Learning New Ways to Collaborate through Action Research

Facilitated by an assistant principal, the first couple of meetings of the newly named Safety Action Research Group (SARG) consisted of opening a dialogue, eliciting the perceived concerns for safety on campus and how to prioritize those concerns, and researching possible strategies to improve safety. At first, the greatest challenge was getting all the members of the group to contribute. A few of them had been so used to looking to others for answers that it took several meetings for them to realize that their contributions were not only valued but needed.

The previous pattern of meetings had trained them to be sitters and getters, and breaking that behavior was an arduous task for the assistant principal who had to prompt and encourage comment while avoiding the temptation to simply solve everything himself. It truly took a group effort to realize that leadership in this setting could not and should not be confined to, or restrained by, formal roles.

Once the group felt comfortable and trusted each other, the dialogue could truly begin. The SARG decided to survey the students and teachers about their safety concerns, examine the history of injury reports, analyze the discipline trends from the previous school year, perform quarterly walkthroughs of the campus, and contact other schools in the district with escalating student populations for their perspectives on school safety.

Since the committee was unanimously concerned with campus-wide supervision of students, the SRO volunteered to research the possibility of a student patrol, something he had heard about at a recent conference. The committee members' willingness to engage in this research both pleased and surprised us.

Through this research, the various members of SARG discovered the predominant safety issues in the school and relevant strategies to address them. As administrators, we were shocked at the extent of existing issues. It was amazing how the simple things like the locations and causes of injury provided us with a new perception of our own supervision of the campus.

In addition to numerous other strategies implemented, SARG developed a new elective class in which two to four students per period supervised the campus to report any safety concerns. Yes, we began a whole new class at the request of SARG! We immediately noticed a reduction in discipline and safety issues.

Although there were a few hiccups along the way, teachers and students alike sang the praises of the new student patrol. Later we discovered that the addition of this elective class provided more than improved supervision, it gave the members of SARG a sense of genuine empowerment and a feeling of impact as advocated by Spreitzer and Quinn. They had indeed made a substantial difference in the broader school community.

Complementing this campus-wide effort and adding to the impact of their work, the SARG set about improving hallway supervision. Like many administrators, we had routinely walked around the hallways to ensure that our teachers adequately supervised the students before school and at transition times. However, the SARG noted there was insufficient hallway supervision and decided that they would address this. But what could they do? The facilitating assistant principal recommended reading a chapter from Rita Stein's *Connecting Character to Conduct: Helping Students Do the Right Things* (2000). From this chapter study, the SARG crafted a pamphlet titled *Hallway Supervision: Safety and Beyond . . . Way Beyond.*

The pamphlet was used to publicize the importance of supervising for safety and extending the curriculum into the hallways. At the request of the SARG, we provided all faculty members with a copy of the pamphlet, asked them to discuss it in their teams, and provided SARG with an opportunity to present the importance of hallway supervision at a faculty meeting. Although this did not result in a miraculous effort by all teachers to be in their doorways every day, it definitely made a noticeable difference.

The Galvanizing Effect on the School Community

The professional behaviors of the SARG had created a schoolwide learning and awareness of why hallway supervision was not simply a task but rather a teaching and learning opportunity. To extend this understanding and sustain the practice, SARG created a team supervision template to be completed by all teams for the following year. The experience of identifying a problem, reviewing literature, writing, sharing, and making structural changes multiplied the SARG members' impact on the community.

It also served as a spark to ignite a fire. We wanted the influence of this pilot action research group to explode all over campus, so in addition to the faculty meeting presentation, we invited the members of SARG to share out at a leadership team meeting. They discussed their work and the process behind their action research. We linked their testimony with the ongoing concept and vocabulary development we had been promoting in our leadership team meetings. This provided team leaders and department heads with a relevant example of the importance of research and associated vocabulary within the context of our school.

Hallway Supervision: Safety & Beyond...Way Beyond

REPORT FOR FACULTY PREPARED BY:
THE SEVEN SPRINGS MIDDLE SCHOOL SAFETY ACTION
RESEARCH GROUP (SARG)

"The hallways offer students a unique mix of instruction, counsel, and discipline."

Rita Stein, et al. (2000)

When considering Maslow's hierarchy of needs, the creation of a safe environment is a necessary prerequisite for meaningful learning. After all, how can students learn when they are worried about being bullied? Unfortunately, the larger and more spread out a school campus gets, the greater the potential for bullying, which can shift victims from a learning mode to a survival mode.

It is amazing how easily our increasingly busy schedules and never ending responsibilities can get in the way of supervising hallways before, after, and in-between classes. Although we cannot be expected to do everything, it would help us to make a paradigm shift.

The traditional purpose of hallway supervision is to serve as a deterrent for inappropriate bullying behaviors. Students are very aware of a teacher's presence and generally behave accordingly. As Rita Stein et al. point out in ***Connecting Character to Conduct***, there is a totally different and much more compelling way to think of hallway supervision. Rather than function as a baby-sitting service, ***"all staff can use non-instructional settings as a natural extension of the written curriculum and instructional focus."*** What better place to apply a social studies lesson regarding the importance of diversity than in the hallway or at the bus loop when a couple of students make fun of another student's differences? Indeed, two of the core beliefs at SSMS are tolerance for differences and diversity as strength.

So called, "non-instructional areas" provide a wonderful and natural "real world" setting to stop these students and let them know how important and positive our differences really are. School faculty can "help students apply guiding principles in settings where students move more freely, adult supervision is less direct, and no formal tasks are involved."

Non-formal areas also include a very important social dynamic of which educators can take advantage. Stein and her co-authors make the point that, **"students have the opportunity to apply the guiding principles as they interact with one another, with teachers, and with other adults in an informal and supportive way. . . . They function as environments that help students better understand themselves, secure a place of importance in their peer group, and make appropriate contact with adults."**

Asking students how they are doing or what they have been up to not only allows them to interact properly and naturally with adults, but also helps develop teacher-student relationships that may be difficult to establish while discussing grammar or fractions.

Think of hall duty as a chance to model . . .

- ➢ **Nurturing behaviors**
- ➢ **Ethical behaviors**
- ➢ **Good citizenship**
- ➢ **Positive social interaction**

I am convinced but I still have a million other things to do . . .

- ➢ **Make a team commitment: each team member could be assigned to one period a day and all should watch in the morning and afternoon.**
- ➢ **Work out a system with a neighboring team to monitor the bathrooms.**
- ➢ **Have a plan for morning meetings: designate one person a month to leave early and monitor the halls or rotate in and out.**
- ➢ **Select one student a month to answer the phone and take messages while you are out monitoring the halls.**
- ➢ **As a team, commit to a tardy policy and stick to it! Consistency is the most effective way!**
- ➢ **Be sure to include hall monitoring as a responsibility within your sub plans!**
- ➢ **Work out a rotation with your co-teacher to monitor the halls.**

Research for this report was completed using:
Stein, R., Richin, R., Banyon, R., Banyon, F., and Stein, M. (2000). *Connecting Character to Conduct: Helping Students Do the Right Things*. Alexandria, VA.: Association for Supervision and Curriculum Development.

Reflecting on This Process

We were so proud of the SARG members. As administrators we had modest expectations for the pilot group but they exceeded our hopes. The SARG demonstrated for the whole faculty the value of professional and collaborative learning through participating in the process of action research. We knew that participation was the key. We learned the barriers this pilot group encountered.

One of the teachers participated at times but often had to be prodded by the administrative facilitator. This teacher either felt ambivalent about the group's work or preferred to be a passive member. At times it seemed he came to the meetings and did a little research solely because of the doughnuts and coffee! This taught us that action research was not something we could force on our faculty and that true empowerment depended partly on a person's desire to be empowered.

On the flip side, the administrative facilitator might have been a little too controlling as he sometimes reverted to functioning as a committee chair. Guidance and leadership are important, but not at the expense of empowerment. It took a few meetings for him to realize that facilitating often means getting out of the way of others, as long as they are focused. This taught us the importance of training teachers and ourselves how to be effective facilitators.

Overall, this first action research group served as a catalyst for change in the culture and climate of the school. Although the lessons learned did not keep us from making mistakes the following year, they definitely convinced us that action research could truly create the professional learning community we had envisioned. When we provided this small group of faculty members with support, freedom, responsibility, and a little bit of guidance, they greatly exceeded our expectations. Now all we needed was to figure out how to encourage the rest of the faculty to participate.

THE JAGUAR JOURNEY

We wanted to support growth from within the school, balanced with support from our professional partnerships. At the end of the school year, the members of SARG shared their results at a leadership meeting. They contrasted their research and action with the decision making and often passive nature of committees. The SARG testimonials underscored the potential to actively impact the school culture and piqued the interest of the teacher leaders in the school.

At the beginning of the next school year, we reached out to our school partners. We invited a professor of education from a local university to present the practices of action research to the entire faculty. At our request he deliberately avoided discussing action research as a philosophy or theory. Instead he provided a practical outline and examples of the benefits from taking part in this type of dynamic structure.

After the presentation, the members of SARG gave a firsthand account of their experiences. Although the results of this pilot group were impressive, it was the personal satisfaction and sense of impact the resonated with the faculty. Great excitement was generated by the SARG members and the professor's presentation.

Developing Schoolwide Interest

Fortunately, this groundswell of interest coincided with a new state initiative that recognized the value of teacher discourse and a mandate for teachers to spend forty minutes per week discussing effective reading strategies. The K–12 Reading Plan could have been viewed negatively as state interference, but given the escalating interest at our school, we viewed this mandate as an opportunity to spread action research.

Middle schools in our district are set up into academic teams, where content area teachers share the same group of students. The forty-minute-per-week mandate called for middle school teachers to meet as teams. This structure fit perfectly with our notions of creating learning communities engaged in action research.

Early on in the new school year we explained the mandate and stated that many school administrators were dictating the weekly reading topics to be discussed. However, we empowered our faculty to decide the important reading issues to focus on. This voluntary process allowed them to meet the mandate through conducting work relevant to the needs of their students.

We also added an incentive to conduct action research by purchasing requested books and materials. Out of the twelve academic teams, nine volunteered to conduct quarterly action research projects. These nine teams were given the Action Research Group binders in which to document their work in process, and each team leader was trained to facilitate a study group by the district's professional development department.

The binders contained templates for writing down identified goals, a log for tracking group progress, a graphic organizer for their cycle of research, and a summary sheet for describing their results and recommendations (see appendix 4.1). The teams that opted out of action research were still required to meet weekly and we provided the topics that needed to be discussed.

Providing opportunities to share their progress beyond the team was critical. To enable this sharing, we set up bimonthly grade level meetings, called Grade Level Activity Sessions. The agenda consisted of teams reporting on their action research topics. Immediately the synergy began, as teachers from different teams started asking for copies of the work so they could implement the strategy on their team. We also employed a teacher who attended all of the activity sessions and produced an action research project progress update (appendix 4.2).

Appendix 4.1 shows an illustrative example of how the whole school faculty stayed informed of the work of each action research group. This allowed successful practices to be shared across all grades and content areas. In addition, promising action research projects were highlighted at leadership meetings and faculty meetings. The shift from a passive faculty to an active one was under way!

FAR FROM PERFECTION

It is important to note that we had a few bumps in the road during our first year of voluntary action research. Teams needed additional support as they struggled with both the research and the implementation of strategies from the research. Sometimes teachers found it difficult to narrow down a focus, and it never ceased to amaze us how a process that should be simple became complicated because of a lack of conceptual understanding.

To take the pulse on the school's work, we invited the professor of education back at the conclusion of the first semester. He met with each action research team without the presence of the administration so that teachers would feel free to be candid in their feedback. At the end of this process he provided us with a report of teacher concerns, including the need for more time to meet and continuous administrative support.

He became a "critical friend" who gave us valuable insight along the way. His passion for teacher-based research to solve student achievement issues served as a constant reminder that administrators cannot solve all of the problems but should encourage those with the greatest knowledge of the students to lead the way. This can be a humbling and challenging experience for an administrator who is accustomed to holding all of the keys, or who oversees a faculty who would prefer to just be told what they should be doing.

THE FIRE IS BURNING

By the second full year of this change process, action research groups became the main structure for learning and evolved as both small group and schoolwide efforts. We provided both cross-grade and grade level meeting structures to allow maximum sharing and learning. Several of these groups made significant improvements in student achievement as highlighted in the teachers' stories in this book.

It was important to us that teachers experience some sense of empowerment through our efforts to foster self-determination. The choice to research, explore, and implement what they felt was best as professional educators had great meaning for them. We supported them by building capacity, providing facilitator training, and giving faculty the time both to research the literature on effective practice and to conduct their own inquiries. This was our effort to help teachers feel confident that they were competent to succeed.

Lastly, we recognized the importance of their research by supporting the implementation of their findings, while celebrating their achievements and the improved student performance in our school. We believe this led to the most important ingredient of true empowerment, a direct impact on students. By making teachers essential to changes in the school culture we were able to improve the climate and how our teachers perceived themselves as professional educators.

EDITORS' DISCUSSION

This chapter confirms the critical role of the school administration. Through their own words the principal and assistant principal (Chris Christoff and Matt Gruhl) teach us all that while authentic professional development and school-based solutions to context-specific problems *might* be possible in any school, when a visionary administration creates a culture of trust and empowerment, that leadership is a catalyst for meaningful change. Chris recognized the steady success of his predecessor but also realized that in order to move the school community forward, he needed to take further initiative.

By recognizing the latest research and the need to act upon those findings, Chris deliberately became a model for his faculty. He quickly realized the power inherent in his actions and began to purposefully mentor his faculty by providing resources, encouraging the sharing of learning, deliberately celebrating success, and promoting further research and reflection.

In this chapter we read a firsthand account of how one successful experience kindled the possibilities for the entire school community and set an example other faculty wished to emulate. We hope that teacher leaders and school principals note that although this takes hard work and a commitment, the changes described in this chapter could happen in *any* school. It is the principal's choice how they use the available human and material resources.

This administrative team did not reinvent education—they simply tried to put current research into practice. They chose to invest in the school faculty and staff and they chose to bring a passion and energy to this work. We hope this inspires other leaders to involve and empower their faculties in finding specific solutions for their schools.

REFERENCES

Spreitzer, G., and Quinn, R. (2001). *A Company of Leaders: Five Disciplines for Unleashing the Power in Your Workforce.* San Francisco: Jossey-Bass.

Stein, R. (2000). *Connecting Character to Conduct: Helping Students Do the Right Things.*

Appendix 4.1: Action Research Group
<u>**Templates for Binders**</u>

Focus Areas/School Improvement Plan Goal(s):

Name of Member	Position at School	Role

Specific goal(s) the group is pursuing for the year:

1.

2.

3.

Research Log

This includes any time reading, analyzing data, and discussions with others, and/or any type of research/inquiry that contributes to the goals of the group. Each member should have his or her own individual log.

Date	Source/Nature of	Summary (attach if necessary)	Time (min)

Action Research Cycle

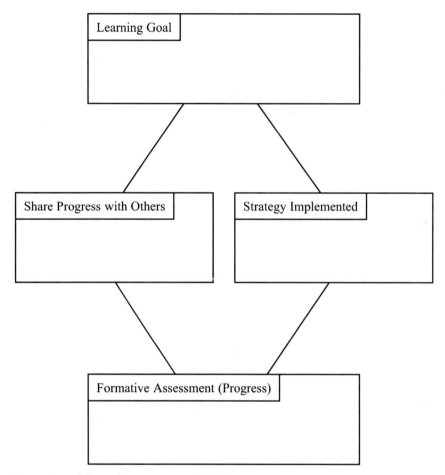

Examples of formative assessment include:

- Pre-test/post-test
- Journal writing
- Responses to Do Now prompts
- Quizzes
- Oral questioning
- Individual conferences
- Student presentations

The following underlined items are grouped together, but each was originally printed separately in order for teachers to have ample space to respond.

<u>Strategies Discovered/Implemented</u>
(Briefly describe how you implemented)

1.
2.
3.
4.

<u>How do you plan to monitor the progress of the strategies implemented?</u>

—

—

—

—

<u>Summative Results</u>
Which strategies worked and which did not work? Include supporting data (quantitative and /or qualitative).

<u>Future Recommendations</u>

Please share your recommendations.

How are you going to share this information with others at the school to improve student learning?

Appendix 4.2
Seven Springs Middle School Schoolwide Action Research Update

Team/ Dept.	Goal	Strategies	Results
6G	(1) Students will increase the number of books in their backpack for silent reading time.	Baseline data of 1st periods books in student possession (fiction & nonfiction).	Student use of nonfiction reading increased.
	(2) Teachers will read articles on co-teaching models to enhance current model.	Articles discussed at team meetings. PD 360—Watched and discussed	
	(3) Interactive Notebooks implemented to aid in student organization and grades.	INBs used in all team classes.	50% of students in reading have made improvement in completing work, note-taking skills, and organization.
	(4) Increase motivation and timely work habits of classwork and homework.	Each teacher selected an area to target to increase motivation: homework completion participation, work quality, etc.	Grades and participation increased significantly in certain classes.
6H	(1) Students will use reading strategies to improve nonfiction comprehension.	Weekly nonfiction reading activities. Teachers will research and implement reading strategies.	21% to 27% were reading nonfiction.
	(2) Students will bring a book to read at all times with hopes that 25% will have nonfiction.	Weekly book check, Media center visits every two weeks, Rewards for reading nonfiction, Media Center presentation—topic nonfiction.	Average score rose to 60% or a 14% increase in nonfiction comprehension.
	(3) Improve writing of a 3.5 paragraph by 25%.	Weekly 3.5 paragraph assignment by team teachers. Teachers will research and implement the writing strategies, outlining, etc.	Writing scores increased an average of 25%.
6J	(1) Various teaching strategies will be used in classrooms.	Team will share learning style strategies and use three during the next two weeks.	

Team/ Dept.	Goal	Strategies	Results
6/7 L	(1) Implementing color with graphic organizers will increase student achievement in all content areas.	Mickey Mouse Graphic Organizer & Highlight text	Student achievement increased in each content area (10%-geography, 4.52%-reading, 5.63%-language arts, 2%-math).
	(2) Students increased their knowledge about reference & research by 25%.	Students will use analysis and evaluation in content areas/Also using reference and research through a media scavenger hunt and the book *Impact*.	The post-test was inconclusive—access to the computer lab did not allow time necessary. Class work collected does demonstrate an improvement in the ability in this area.
	(3) Free time will be offered as a reward for turning in all assignments.	Two tickets were given to each student and then taken back for each assignment not turned in.	No improvement in the amount of turned in work.
7C	(1) At least 25% of students choose to read nonfiction during default to reading time.	Weekly book checks, rewards for students reading nonfiction, media center visit every two weeks, a wide variety of nonfiction books will be available on team.	There was a 56% increase in nonfiction reading by end of year.
	(2) Increase student scores by increasing parent contact and involvement.	Teacher contact with parents concerning behavior and underachievement. Increase parent/teacher conferences. Winter celebration breakfast to promote parent/teacher camaraderie.	Low performing students experienced increased success.
	(3) Boost student motivation with emphasis on struggling students.	Enlist guidance and SSAP/More progress reports when needed/parent contact/student behavior sheets as appropriate/rewards.	Marginal success was noted/team states that one quarter was not enough time to carry out this goal.
	(4) Reduce the amount of bullying (physical & verbal).	Language Arts Unit on peer pressure/Team Teachers, guidance and SSAP counsel students/parent contact.	
7D	Increase amount of nonfiction reading.	Tied to Harvest Reading Festival; backpack checks; media visit	Increase of 11% more nonfiction reading.

Team/ Dept.	Goal	Strategies	Results
7F	Motivate students to maintain academic focus for Quarter 4.	Reward system: Biweekly field day	This reward system did not motivate the students as hoped.
8A	(1) Increase sentence writing skills of responses to content area question.	Focus & instruction through language arts of complex sentences/ Student copies of checklists and posters for classrooms/practice provided for written response questions.	14% improvement of level 2's 7% decrease of level 1's 7% decrease of level 0's
	(2) 75% of students will improve their note-taking skills as measured by results of open note tests.	Direct instruction in taking and organizing notes.	100% increase from pre-test to post -test
8B	(1) Increase student vocabulary.	Word of the day in each class.	85% of the students mastered the words given.
	(2) Improve student research techniques.	Class project focusing on data acquisition and interpretation.	
8E	(1) Increase proficiency of critical analysis skills.	Teachers will incorporate high level questions in classroom activities and use action words from Bloom's Taxonomy.	
	(2) Increase motivation for homework and classwork completion.	Rewards by class for better grades/homework for the week assigned at one time/research and math projects.	90% of students turned in a research paper; previously 70% of students turned in homework.
Gifted	(1) Students will improve reading proficiency.	Nonfiction reading assigned every Monday and Friday. Summarize one article a week.	
ESE	(1) 90% of students pursuing special standards will score in proficient range as measured by new alternate assessment for special diploma.	Training in alternate assessment (new state version) for all teachers.	

Team/ Dept.	Goal	Strategies	Results
Fine Arts	(1) Implement strategies such as graphic or vocabulary strategies to improve literacy.	Use of graphic organizers promoted through weekly meetings.	
	(2) Increased parent involvement.	Send home postcards each quarter with positive comments. Create websites for parent accessibility and involvement.	Each teacher created a website by the end of the school year.
CTE	(1) Team will match the 30 competencies from the Middle School Career Academic Advisement from the DOE.	Correlating with career target nonfiction research and college exploration note-taking.	Coin books completed.
	(2) CTE will improve essential writing skills to 3.3 on the FCAT Writes.	Nonfiction research, college note-taking, graphic organizers, peer editing, composition format.	School score raised to 4.3.
Math Dept.	(1) Students will increase classroom participation and completion of homework during first quarter.	Utilze activities that specifically add sports and music.	80% baseline. Check 1: 92.8% Check 2: 91.2% Check 3: 97.5%
Sci. Dept.	8th grade students will increase science proficiency.	Use of pre- and post-tests created by science department.	

III

PRACTITIONER RESEARCH CHAPTERS

5

Coming Full Circle

Describing a Year of Action Research

Leslie Frick

Leslie Frick invites us into her first experiences using action research with differentiated instruction. She writes of her motivations, the pre-planning, and the initial processes using action research to guide her teaching and makes some practical suggestions to help teachers begin.

It's nearly the end of a school year, just a few weeks before the kids are "out of here"; our summer vacation plans are arranged, and our classroom is almost packed up. It is then that our minds begin to wander to the upcoming school year . . . August, looking at all of those new faces with so much potential. The possibilities are endless. Even after eighteen years of teaching I feel the excitement that a new school year brings.

Come on. Admit it. You know you do it. As corny as it sounds, you begin to think about next school year. How can you make it better? Can it be more interesting, more exciting, and yes, more meaningful for the students?

We were hearing buzz about "action research." It seemed like it was everywhere. We learned about it at conferences, through teacher journals, and now from our administration. Our administrators were fresh out of their master's program in educational leadership, and much of what they had been learning about was the use of data in curriculum and instructional planning. I thought, "Time. Great idea, but never enough time."

Our principal asked our school leadership team to think about trying to implement action research in the upcoming school year. I'm always willing to try something new. It's good to keep things fresh. It may not always work, but this made sense. Use the data to drive instruction. But what data? What research? How do I pick just one thing?

That's when I began looking through the many books on the shelf I never had time to read thoroughly and found one on differentiated instruction. The book, by Carol Ann Tomlinson, was entitled *How to Differentiate Instruction in Mixed-Ability Classrooms.* I'd always wanted to implement differentiated instruction strategies in middle school, but hadn't quite had the time to figure it out.

When I taught elementary school, differentiated instruction was a way of life. Every child was at a different place in their development and needed an individualized plan to help them take the next step. My thoughts began to wander, thinking back to all of the reasons why differentiated instruction worked and I wanted to make this work here in middle school as well.

Suggestion # 1: Pick something that inspires you and interests you. That way the time you invest will be time well spent.

THE CLOSE OF THE PRECEDING SCHOOL YEAR

I didn't really think about other team members joining in. I just knew I wanted to start. On our final planning day before the summer break I looked at the small stack of books on a student desk ready for my summer reading. The science teacher on our team came into my classroom, saw the differentiated instruction book on top of the stack, and started thumbing through it. We began to discuss part of the book, why I wanted to read it, and some ideas I had for action research. I can't remember exactly how it happened, but by the end of the conversation, she took a second copy I had packed up and we both agreed to read it and get together in July to discuss it.

Suggestion # 2: Talk about your ideas. There will usually be somebody who is interested in the same topic. Having someone along for the ride makes it more enjoyable as well.

I took a few weeks off to decompress from the year's activities, enjoy some time with the family, and complete some projects around the house. At the beginning of July I pulled out my stack of books and began reading the book on differentiated instruction. I couldn't put it down. I was making notes in the columns, tabbing ideas I wanted to remember, and applying it to the subject I was teaching in the next school year.

At the end of each chapter I typed up some notes to accompany the book so that when I read the information during the upcoming school year I could find it more easily. We all know that once the school year gets into full swing, we never have enough time.

Suggestion # 3: Organize your information into a format that you can quickly reference during the school year. You'll save yourself a great deal of time and will be more willing to implement ideas if you have them at your fingertips.

PLANNING THROUGH THE SUMMER

About the middle of July I met with the science teacher on our team. We spent a morning with our books, a long list of notes, a wonderful homemade dessert, and a fresh pitcher of raspberry iced tea. (What teacher isn't able to better concentrate with good food to snack on? It's all about the food!) We were both excited about what we had read. We were full of ideas, and before we knew it three hours had passed. We developed a plan to implement some ideas on our team. For now it would be just in our two classrooms. We hoped the other teachers would like what they saw and be willing to buy into what we were doing, but we would have to wait and see.

Our approaches were totally different. I wanted to establish differentiated stations once a week based on the social studies curriculum, and she wanted to create an independent study program with options for each child based on their interests and ability. The important thing to note was that it was okay to implement different ideas. Our actions didn't have to be the same.

Both of us planned to try strategies mentioned in the book we had been reading, but we allowed each other the freedom to adapt them in a way that best suited our classroom, content, and teaching style. Our ultimate goal was to generate time to work with students either individually or in small groups in order to clarify concepts they had difficulty understanding after initial instruction. Both of these plans allowed for that.

Suggestion # 4: Select the goal you are trying to accomplish as a group and allow each member to decide how to implement the strategy in their own classroom. This will provide teachers the freedom and creativity they are used to having, and it will keep tension at a minimum because you're not trying to have everyone conform to one standard.

Following our first get-together I began to look at the upcoming year's curriculum and decided that Fridays would be the best day to pull students for additional support and instruction. I was energized and ready to write plans during the summer. These were going to be the most fabulous, engaging, creative, and differentiated activities anyone had ever seen!

Within days, I found myself attempting to plan multiple suggestions from the book and started to feel overwhelmed. I needed to stop and think, so I put my plans away for a few days. Then I took some time to review the notes I had jotted down while reading. I quickly noticed the laundry list of ideas had become my version of CliffsNotes, and I realized I was trying to do too much too soon. I wasn't heeding the advice repeatedly stated throughout the book.

Differentiated instruction isn't something you do. It's a philosophy. It's a way of teaching. It's a process. Differentiated instruction takes time to implement, and it doesn't have to be done all at once. It was such an "Aha!" moment that I immediately felt relief. Right then and there I took a deep breath and gave myself permission to take it slow, knowing that if I became overwhelmed, I might not be able to follow through. I decided this was too important to not follow through.

Suggestion # 5: Give yourself permission to take it slow. You won't accomplish anything if you become overwhelmed and fail to follow through.

After this revelation it was time for the next step. It was important to address different modalities and create a variety of activities, as those were suggested ways to *begin* differentiating instruction. This was a *reasonable* place to start. I searched for nine activities that could reinforce or enrich the content, could be completed in forty minutes, and had reading, writing, listening, and/ or higher order thinking included. Nine activities allowed for one station every week of the nine-week quarter.

There were stations that utilized technology, some that were product based, some that promoted inquiry, and some that highlighted an aspect of the culture of the continent being studied. This required up-front work, but once it was done, it was smooth sailing until the next quarter. After setting more realistic expectations I was pleasantly surprised that the time involved was less than I anticipated.

Suggestion # 6: Look at your curriculum guidelines and your school calendar. Address concepts to be covered during the quarter and use the stations for reinforcement, enrichment, and/or review. That way if the student is pulled for grouping, they won't be missing out on the required content already taught and will be extending and refining their learning

**while working at the station. Previewing the school calendar will remove
surprises, such as school being out three out of the next nine Fridays,
and ensure you won't spend time on unnecessary planning. Remember
we're always trying to use our time wisely.**

THE NEW SCHOOL YEAR

Before I knew it, August had arrived. It was the first day back and the faculty
was all abuzz greeting one another and catching up on the summer's festivi-
ties. Everyone was refreshed, renewed, and ready to start the year. The science
teacher and I quickly reconnected and were excited to implement our plans.

The Principal's Guidance

Our principal introduced action research to the entire staff during the first
faculty meeting of pre-planning. Teams were encouraged to look at student
data and consider possible strategies to improve their performance. The school
administration wanted teachers to research together, share information, implement strategies, and collect data to analyze the results. The hook was that if we
participated we could earn in-service points for recertification. Two of us on
our team were already on board. Could we get the others to join in?

Later that afternoon our team was meeting to prepare for the upcoming
schoolwide registration day. The morning's topic of action research naturally
came up during our conversation, and I decided to talk about the book I had
read over the summer. The science teacher and I both shared our plans, and
our teammates felt they could begin to explore differentiated strategies in
their classrooms. They agreed to jump on board, but for very different reasons. One teacher was simply looking for in-service points while the other
really liked the concept. That was okay. We were on the same page and we
were going to help our kids. I wasn't concerned about the motives at this
point. I was just glad we were all going to work toward a common goal.

**Suggestion # 7: It's okay if people join your group for different reasons.
They will all learn something about the topic and hopefully implement
some new strategies. Isn't that the ultimate goal?**

I spoke to our principal the next afternoon; he agreed to purchase additional
copies of the book for the other teachers and they arrived approximately

a week later. We established a *reasonable* reading schedule spending two weeks on each chapter—one week to read and digest the information, and one week to discuss it as a group. The team decided to meet in our common planning times on Wednesday afternoons for thirty minutes. This way the time spent sharing would not become too burdensome and a definite ending time already existed. We brought our books with our highlights and notes and just shared what we learned in a relaxed and comfortable atmosphere.

Sometimes we'd bring a snack to share (remember food brings people together). The atmosphere needed to remain positive and we had high hopes of improving our teaching skills and our students' learning.

Suggestion # 8: Create a reasonable research schedule and time to share what you've learned. Bring a snack and make the time enjoyable. It will make you happy and build a good team atmosphere. It's time well spent. Take time to nourish your craft (individually and/or as a group) or you risk becoming one of those stale, grumpy old teachers just counting the days until retirement. May that never happen!

ORGANIZING WITH DATA

During the planning week, I accessed the student data from the previous year's Florida Comprehensive Assessment Test (FCAT). I was able to see each student's reading and math levels and soon would have beginning-of-year baseline data from our Lexile reading scores and initial writing samples. I broke the information down class by class and quickly learned the makeup in each class was very different. Some classes needed strategies others didn't need.

The goal was to find out what each class needed and use that information to drive the instruction. Then I would see what specific students needed and use the time during stations on Friday to provide more individualized instruction.

The first week of the quarter was spent organizing all of this data and finishing up the prep work for the quarter's station activities. Friday was spent explaining the rationale of differentiated instruction to the students. I demonstrated how each station worked and what students would be doing when I pulled them for small group or individual instruction. The first goal was to create an atmosphere that was nonthreatening.

Students had to understand this wasn't just "the dumb kids" getting extra help. They had to realize that we all need help sometimes, no matter where we are in our learning, and I was going to take the time every Friday to help them with their particular needs. Some students were a little apprehensive and some were elated. Some were glad to have time to socialize with their friends while they were working and others felt that if they were pulled to work with me, then they were getting out of doing some other work and that was fine with them!

I had no idea how much my students would need my help this year. After sifting through the pages of data I soon found out the majority of our students were well below grade level expectation in reading, writing, and math. At the same time, I had students functioning well above grade level expectations. My focus on differentiated instruction couldn't have come at a more opportune time. These kids needed this.

Suggestion # 9: Taking time to look at the data will give you a new perspective on your students. I promise you it is time well spent. It only took me a few hours to analyze four different sets of data, create a chart to organize the information into a "teacher friendly" format, and discover the areas of need for each of my five classes.

ADAPTING INSTRUCTION TO MEET STUDENT NEEDS

The data revealed the majority of students needed help with main idea and comprehension, so that's where I began. Every other week students discussed current events in class. We went over how to highlight the main ideas when reading each article and how to summarize the information clearly and completely. The Friday before their assignments were due, I pulled students who struggled with the concept of main idea and I reviewed an additional example with them. While I worked with these students, the others were completing the independent activities created to support the unit of study.

I looked over the grades of the current events and pulled students who struggled with the activity, showed them examples of exemplary work, and gave them the opportunity to complete the assignment again for a higher grade. Unfortunately, only half of the students redid the assignment. Every student who resubmitted the assignment showed improvement, but as I would soon learn, many of my students had more to deal with after the 2:50 dismissal bell than current events. I would need to try something else for those who failed to redo the assignment.

Suggestion # 10: Don't be disappointed if what you try doesn't work or doesn't achieve the result you desired. Take the time to figure out why it didn't meet your expectations and adjust. That's not failure. It's adaptation. Remember that your ultimate goal is to help the students.

The next week I talked with the students who didn't try to find out why they hadn't. During first period I received blank stares and "I don't knows." That got me nowhere, so I decided to speak with students individually during my next class and boy, did I get an earful! I heard about having to babysit a sibling so Mom could go to work, not wanting to go home because no one was there, and a few didn't care about their grades because they had the misconception they would be promoted whether they passed or failed. This scared me because it was only week three of school and I would teach them for the next two years. (At this school we stay with the same students for seventh and eighth grade.)

I tried a different approach with this group and offered them several options: Use Fridays to complete work they couldn't get done at home, come in before school, or work during their lunch. A zero for the assignment wasn't going to be an option. Educating them was not only my job but theirs also, and they were robbing themselves of their right to an education if they chose not to do the work. I knew these students with poor grades and low FCAT scores would need some assistance in rethinking their approach to their studies.

I enlisted the help of a new assistant principal and she was more than willing to back up my statements. Not only did she pull them down to her office for a little heart-to-heart conversation, she followed up with them to see how their assignments were coming. This was done during informal visits to our class, stopping them in the hallway for a quick chat, and even in the lunchroom during her lunch duty. Her extra attention made a great deal of impact on five students in particular.

Suggestion # 11: Get to know your students. Really know your students. Find out what makes them tick, why they are struggling, and let them know you're there for them. They'll go the extra mile for you, if they know you care. Let your administration and/or support staff know what you're doing and enlist their support. They are more than willing to help.

LOOKING BACK ON THAT FIRST YEAR

Each week after that, I spent a half an hour looking over work samples, grades, and test scores to see who needed additional help. At the end of the first quarter only 11 percent of the students had a failing average. This was the lowest number I had experienced as a teacher and I was ecstatic! I addressed a new need that was different for each class. We had better weeks than others and better quarters than others, but in the end I learned that analyzing data worked for my students. I worked differently than I had ever worked. Not harder, just differently.

By the end of May I was as tired as usual after forty weeks of the school year, but I also felt greatly rewarded knowing that nearly all of our students showed growth based on either grades, exit reading tests, or standardized tests. Many joined the ranks of being "on grade level." Many students improved beyond the one-year expected growth and one student gained nearly three years of growth in one year. That was amazing to me! I found something else that worked and something else to add to my little bag of tricks. The year was quite a success!

Differentiation continues to be the philosophy that guides my instruction, and each year I add new ways to differentiate the curriculum in order to meet the needs of the students with whom I have the privilege to work. Action research has led me into other areas of interest, such as learning about *The Ten Different Students You'll Meet in Your Classroom,* to help better connect with my students.

This upcoming year I'm looking into previewing and accelerating strategies to use with students. There is a great deal of research in that area and some proven strategies that help catch kids up. It's June and I'll take the next few weeks off. In July, I'll begin gearing up for another exciting year with the students. As we all know, August will be here before we know it. We'll begin a new year with so much potential. Ahh, the possibilities are endless!

EDITORS' DISCUSSION

Leslie Frick's account shows us that professional development truly is a process. After eighteen years she still sought new avenues to extend her teaching and described how she thinks about teaching year-round. This is a candid story of her learning process and the ways in which her administration supported her efforts. In this chapter she speaks to other teachers through her suggestions—honest and realistic thoughts that give us a window into the daily life of her classroom and the actions she took to strengthen her craft.

This chapter also illustrates how teachers can examine data to respond to the needs of their students. Leslie describes how she had to find multiple ways to address the students' learning and the deliberate efforts she made to build relationships, both with the students and her colleagues.

Leslie closes the chapter by reporting the academic success of her students. This is indeed the benchmark by which she will be judged as an effective teacher in this state. We, however, wish to stress that the standardized success of her students is just the tip of the proverbial iceberg. In these critical middle school years, she opened doors for students who had very limited success before.

Through her encouragement and sound instruction she had built their confidence and, we hope, their resiliency to continue investing in their own education. In turn, even after eighteen years of teaching, Leslie came to better understand her students' lives. This chapter confirms that teachers who challenge themselves *will* make a difference.

REFERENCES

Gill, Vickie. (2007). *The Ten Different Students You'll Meet in Your Classroom: Classroom Management Tips for Middle and High School Teachers.* Thousand Oaks, CA: Corwin Press.

Tomlinson, Carol Ann. (2001). *How to Differentiate Instruction in Mixed-Ability Classrooms.* Alexandria, VA: Association for Supervision and Curriculum Development.

6

Service Learning and Action Research

Developing a Course that Sparked the Flame of Citizenship

Cindy Tehan and Janet Tolson

*In this chapter Cindy Tehan and Janet Tolson describe one re-
markable initiative using service learning as the foundation for
student-based action research. The results were impressive and
thought-provoking for the students, teachers, and administration
at Seven Springs Middle School.*

In the past Seven Springs Middle Schools (SSMS) has been the recipient
of a Florida Learn and Serve grant. Originally, this grant funded character
building through drama and chorus productions. However in the spring of
2006 the grant closed. In order to continue receiving the funding, SSMS
needed to seek a new direction.

To help with this initiative an action research team was formed comprised
of four guidance counselors, a chorus teacher, a graphic arts teacher, a reading teacher, a computer teacher, a drama teacher, and one assistant principal. Working as a collaborative community we examined the needs of the
student body and the new requirements of this grant. We discussed many
possibilities such as whether to work with local community organizations or
the neighboring high school.

We met with Joe Follman, the Florida Learn and Serve director. I mentioned that I found it most successful to keep my work within SSMS.
Several previous forays into working with other schools had been less than
satisfactory, partially due to insufficient buy-in by other schools' administration. Mr. Follman suggested a youth council. A youth council is a group
of students who read, evaluate, and determine monetary awards for multiple
service learning projects. They begin with a set amount of funds ($5,000 to

$7,000) and then request grant proposals from classes and clubs who wish to perform service-learning projects, awarding $50 to $500 to each proposal.

This idea complemented our initial analysis of a student survey given to three randomly chosen classes in the previous spring. Eighty-five percent of the students responded "agree" or "strongly agree" to the statement "I like to help people." However, only 40 percent responded "agree" or "strongly agree" to the statement "I can make a difference in my community." This data suggested to us that students wanted to help others but did not have a framework in which to work. If we were to open the grant to the whole school, we might help students realize they can make a difference in their community.

OVERCOMING OBSTACLES

The fundamental key to promoting the success of service learning was the formation of a leadership class that functions as a youth council. During initial planning, our action research group considered the feasibility of a club to meet the needs of the school. Students could be involved in a variety of projects that the club sponsored.

It became apparent that a club meeting once per week would not provide students with enough time and experience to learn the intricate processes and decision making necessary to manage a $9,000 grant. Students would require training and expertise to manage and make decisions on such a large sum, and they would also require an in-depth knowledge of the concept of service learning.

During an action research meeting, the graphic arts teacher, who had previous administrative experience, recognized the need for an established class to conduct service learning. Our assistant principal pursued the possibility of formation of a class. State coding of the new class caused some concerns. With a focus on the function of the class, the decision was made to code the class as an elective under research as the students would be conducting their own investigatory studies. With support from our principal, the class was approved and named Lead the Pack (LTP) and designed to promote leadership roles for students within our school and our community.

A student survey demonstrated to us that our students had a high desire to assist others, but very few students felt that one person could make a difference. There seemed to be no outlet for them to put their generosity and concern for others into action. We advertised the class with a strong emphasis on community involvement, leadership, and making a difference. The advertising approach appealed to students and interest in the class began to grow.

Once the class was established, we focused on the selection of students. Ms. Tehan agreed to teach the class. She felt very strongly that all students should have an opportunity to apply for the class. Unlike other electives, the leadership class would require an application with a written essay. Approximately twenty-five students from across the academic spectrum applied and were admitted to the class.

LEAD THE PACK TAKES FORM

After a great deal of research we sought input and support from a University of South Florida professor with expertise in service learning. Ms. Tehan began to structure a curriculum and expectations. A syllabus was generated.

Demystifying the Grant Writing Process

The students would learn how to write, evaluate, manage, oversee, and document the progress of grants. To learn these sophisticated skills Ms. Tehan decided the class should begin by creating their own grant. Mr. Follman returned to instruct students on the components of service learning. Cathryn Berger Kaye's book, *The Complete Guide to Service Learning,* was chosen as the class text. For the first year, the students wrote a grant titled, "Good Habits, Good Health," designed to teach exercise and nutrition to elementary school students and SSMS sixth graders.

Next, students throughout the school were invited to work with a teacher sponsor and apply for mini-grants of up to $500.00. Two students from each class in the school were released to come to the service learning class to write the grant with LTP mentors who would help to explain the process.

Each group of students wrote the framework of their grant. The grant was then returned to the sponsoring teacher for editing and final submission. This process proved to be confusing to the student writers and their sponsoring teachers as everyone learned information was required. As a result Ms. Tehan's class learned a great deal from this experience and streamlined the application guidelines and the writing process for the future.

Evaluating the Grant Proposals

After grants were submitted, the LTP class had to review each grant and to determine if a substantial amount of service learning was involved and whether to fund the grant. For instance, Ms. Tolson, who was on this action research team and a sponsoring teacher, did not include some components required on the grant application. She submitted the grant based on the information her two students shared with her, but did not know to include cross-referencing to the state standards.

Students in the LTP class were then faced with the dilemma. The grant could be a good one but did not meet the required criteria. Two LTP students, one a former pupil of Ms. Tolson's, were selected to explain to her that her grant would only be considered if revisions were made. One can only imagine the trepidation a student would experience going to a teacher to say, "I'm sorry, but this is not quite good enough. We would like you to resubmit your grant."

Ms. Tehan was a little nervous about how teachers would receive a critique from students about their grants. She telephoned teachers in advance to let them know that the students were coming and to alert them to the corrections that would be required. This alert turned out to be a pretty savvy move on the part of Ms. Tehan, as it gave time for teachers to review their grant proposals and then understand what the students were attempting to communicate. As it was still early in the year, the students' communication skills had not been honed, and they were nervous and uncertain about this step in the process.

The experience of approaching a former teacher and professionally stating that the grant would require additional information was particularly validating for the students. They began to develop real-world communication skills as they presented the information and negotiated possible solutions. The action research team concluded that this autonomy was a crucial step in the process. The students became personally attached and invested in the approval process for their grants.

The Benefits for Students

Evaluating the grants promoted decision making and an adherence to stated requirements. It provided students with a new perspective for the necessity of rules as now *they*, and not their teachers, were responsible for seeing the rules were followed. By the second year of grant submissions, the students had developed thoroughness in evaluating each proposal. There was even a comical moment that illustrated their attention to detail when they initially denied Ms. Tehan a grant for character education because she forgot to sign it. She had to resubmit the grant proposal!

Students also developed understanding and compassion for first-time grant writers. They often voted to extend a deadline for a worthy project and provided more support to the teacher and students who had not previously undergone the process. Students developed a high degree of responsibility while balancing compassion, cooperation, and criticism. Their emerging skills in communication, work habits, and standards for accomplishment impacted student performance in other areas of their academic and personal lives.

SHARING THE VISION

Teams of LTP students were assigned to document the progress of each project. These teams created backboard displays and scrapbooks and documented the performance of the projects on film along with interviews of teachers and participants. Problems occasionally arose with scheduling as LTP students had to interview or film grant projects outside the LTP class meeting time. Teachers across the school agreed to excuse LTP from their classes but only if the students' work was up to date and met the teacher's standards of performance. Consequently, LTP students learned very quickly that being caught up or ahead in all their classes would be a necessity for their success in both the Lead the Pack class and their other classes.

In addition, every LTP student learned the technological aspects of video taping, digital photography, and computer programs to create movies and PowerPoint presentations. Some difficulties occurred when students needed the same equipment simultaneously. The school district media director worked with the students several times to help them refine their techniques so that they could produce a high-caliber presentation.

The students successfully presented their projects to the Middle School Design Team at the school district level. They presented to several legislators in at the state capital in Tallahassee during Earth Day celebrations and were recognized by State Senator Mike Fasano for an environmental project to protect Sandhill Cranes. The program has enjoyed enormous success during its second year with many of the obstacles from the first year resolved.

A CASE STUDY: PROTECTING THE SANDHILL CRANE

Two eighth grade students, Matt and Jake, came to Ms. Tehan. They were concerned that the sandhill cranes on the busy Trinity Boulevard were getting killed by the cars and wanted to research how to have signs posted warning, "Sandhill Crane Crossing." Ms. Tehan suggested Matt and the rest

of the class could make a series of phone calls, identifiying themselves as students at SSMS and leaving a school number for return calls. I told them they would need to find out who is in charge of this and ask what it takes to post a new sign.

With that, the students started phoning county commissioners, state representatives, state senators, mayors, the Audubon Society, among others. Just two days later, the phone rang in my classroom and a man's voice asked to speak to Matt. This man identified himself as State Senator Fasano. He wanted to help Matt with this project. The senator told Ms. Tehan that the roads in question were county roads and that he would write a letter to the county commissioner to ask for the signs.

While she had the senator on the phone, Ms. Tehan invited him to speak with the class about how laws are made and to give out awards to the students involved in service learning. He agreed. During his visit he reminded the students that every law begins with an idea just like theirs and was so supportive of their active citizenship. This event was covered by the local newspapers and the TV stations.

Weeks later, three "Wildlife Area" signs were posted on community roads. Although these did not specify "Sandhill Cranes," they did alert motorists to the nature around them. The students were satisfied as they felt that the sign included tortoises as well as cranes. Our principal then worked with our plant manager to create signs that said, "Sandhill Crane Crossing" and three of these signs were posted on the school campus. This brought a positive response from so many community members. The LTP students received phone calls, e-mails, and comments from students, teachers, and community leaders.

The idea that students do have a voice, that they can make an important difference, became reality through this action research project. The students also entered their work in "Project Citizen," a national contest to promote citizenship, and earned second in the state for their efforts. They presented and defended their project in Orlando before three judges and were praised for their active civic engagement.

Providing students with an avenue to help others is a very rewarding endeavor. The students learn the joy of making a difference in other people's lives and hopefully, this will become a lifelong healthy habit. The initial research showed that the students have a desire to be helpful but not always a way to do it. The Lead the Pack class with the help of the Florida Learn and Serve grant was able to provide students with the means to make a difference and they flew with it. We collected data to show the impact of the project and report our results to the funding agency, as you can see in table 6.1.

Table 6.1   Project Report

Florida Learn and Serve Grant Project Report: Lead the Pack

Lead the Pack (LTP) is an exceptional student-led program at Seven Springs Middle School (SSMS). In 2006–2007 ($8,000) and again in 2007–2008 ($9,000), SSMS received a grant award from the state of Florida Learn and Serve Program that allowed the students to award mini-grants to nine projects throughout the school. These projects then served the community in areas from tutoring to character education to environmental preservation to multiple sclerosis awareness. Not only did these twenty-three students empower the students and teachers of our school to address community needs, but the twenty-three students themselves made significant improvement on their FCAT scores. Thus, we have a program that creates **citizen scholars!**

The following data shows a correlation between the *LTP* class and success on the FCAT:

Percentage of Increase in FCAT Achievement Levels
Reading

Students in Lead the Pack Class	38%
SSMS Students	18%

Mathematics

Students in Lead the Pack Class	14%
SSMS Students	6.3%

Over twenty faculty members and administrators are involved in the many community service projects that this class promotes.

Perhaps much of the academic growth can be attributed to the empowerment of our students. The students determine who will and who will not receive the grant awards. They base their decisions on established criteria that award points to each section of the mini-grant proposals. They then work with the grantees to encourage project success, and they track and record successes with display boards and iMovies.

LESSONS LEARNED

Now that we have several years' experience with a LTP youth council, we can reflect on lessons learned over time. Trust was the first lesson that the students taught us. We provided instruction and leadership opportunities, and then we had to step back and let the students take over. That loss of control is a frightening feeling for teachers, but the students always come through. Even when the tasks seemed unattainable, the students rose to the occasion.

Responsibility was another huge lesson. The students gradually assumed all responsibility for the direction and production of the class. While the students had rigorous assignments and requirements, they also had a sense of accomplishment. Their sense of responsibility and autonomy flowed over into other subject areas. By taking charge of their learning in the LTP class, they found more direction in other aspects of their lives.

Our school administration and teachers agreed to the formation of the LTP class without setting limitations on the expectations. The class was very fluid in its early days as we tested the possibilities of what could be achieved. This open "no limits" perspective permitted students to reach higher and plan more broadly than we had previously foreseen. Our students constantly astounded us with their creativity, ingenuity, and intellect. They found new ways to solve problems and matured as they handled the problems that arose.

They really impressed us with the sophisticated level of response incorporated into their presentations. Sometimes it was difficult, and still is, for us to remember that they are only seventh and eighth grade students! These achievements led the faculty on the action research team to invite two students to join with three faculty on an evaluation subcommittee. We have now expanded the leadership positions for students at our school through the formation of groups such as Student Council.

The greatest impression on the teachers was observing the broad range and impact of the service-learning projects. Students, who had previously felt they had no outlet to assist others and very few options to make a difference, have begun to do just that. Our students now correspond by using Skype (video conferencing) with other schools across the nation to help them with their service learning.

Students are actively involved with organizations such as the National Multiple Sclerosis Society, the American Association of University Women, the Society for the Prevention of Cruelty to Animals, and many others. We believe that our students have begun to view themselves as global citizens who contribute to the world beyond their day-to-day personal lives. Lead the

Pack has shown them that they can make a difference in their community, their nation, their world—all through making a difference in their actions within their personal lives.

EDITORS' DISCUSSION

Never underestimate visionary teachers! Cindy Tehan and Janet Tolson were prepared to take a risk with their curriculum and involve their students in a grand experiment. Their story reminds us that when administrators neutralize the risks and encourage teachers to be creative with the curriculum, teaching becomes a living process. It is true that this chapter describes an elective class; nonetheless, Cindy and Janet structured an environment that would focus the children on discrete outcomes, but then allowed the students to pursue the learning process in authentic and personally meaningful ways.

Through this chapter we appreciate that it takes time and effort to focus children on extensions of the curriculum that build real-world competencies and higher-level critical skills. If school doesn't appear to be relevant to students, then who is to blame? How do we identify, propose, and then use unorthodox resources to enhance the attributes we *know* our students will need in this century? Teachers need assistance finding a professional context where they feel comfortable extending the basic curriculum and "stepping out of the box." Cindy and Janet's experience reveals that a culture of inquiry is one such context.

REFERENCE

Kaye, Cathryn Berger. (2003). *The Complete Guide to Service Learning: Proven, Practical Ways to Engage Students in Civic Responsibility, Academic Curriculum, and Social Action.* Minneapolis, MN: Free Spirit Publishing.

7

Action Research? You've Got to Be Kidding Me

Danielle Lawrence

Danielle Lawrence is very honest about her hesitancy taking on a new initiative. Like many teachers, she was already pressed for time and felt overwhelmed by the idea of adding action research to her teaching responsibilities. This chapter outlines how Danielle came to accept and then embrace a new approach to her teaching.

When the concept of action research was introduced to our school a few years ago, I was working in a self-contained special education (ESE) classroom on a team with three other teachers. We were teaching a group of students who were working toward a regular diploma in grades six through eight, who exhibited varying exceptionalities and the academic abilities of third or fourth graders. Given this population, we did not jump on the action research bandwagon and did the bare minimum at first.

SKEPTICISM AND HESITANCY

We were all very dedicated to the progress of our students, don't get me wrong, but formally meeting for an hour a week to discuss data and progress was just something we believed we did not have time to do. Luckily for us, our ESE team worked under the premise of "you leave us alone, we'll leave you alone" and we worked very self-sufficiently. However, when another local middle school opened, all but two of the students on our ESE team transferred and we were left wondering where we would be teaching next year.

The next year, for the first time in my teaching career, I found myself work-ing on a regular education team as an ESE co-teacher with a whole new set of expectations—including action research. It has been quite a journey, and we have learned quite a bit about each other, our students, and ourselves!

Our new team was going to be sharing a group of seventh grade students. Five teachers, all with different personalities, ideas, backgrounds, and teach-ing styles, came together for the first time to help 140 twelve-year-olds make academic gains. Our biggest obstacle in the beginning was simply, "How are we going to do this?" How does a professional group of teachers put their personal differences aside for the benefit of student improvement? Of course that was something we had always done on our own, but working together with one common goal sounded . . . well . . . difficult.

We stumbled our way through our first few learning goal cycles, but quite honestly, it was on the back burner for many of us. Personally, it was my first year as an ESE co-teacher and I was trying to find my way through a maze of paperwork, lesson plans, and differing teaching styles of my four content area teammates. By the third quarter (marked by the pressures of FCAT test-ing), I had an overall feeling of "Who cares? I don't have time for this!" At that most inopportune time our team leader stepped down and I decided in spite of myself to apply for her position. Together we fumbled through the rest of our first year—promising each other and ourselves that the next year would be better.

OVERCOMING OUR DOUBTS AND FEARS

That leads us to this year. Our school loops from seventh to eighth grade and so we had the advantage of continuing with the same group of students. However, two of our five teachers were new to the team. In some ways we were starting from scratch and in other ways we were right on track. We decided to focus on developing the reading proficiency of our students based on their responses to the Essential Questions associated with each unit of study. For us, choosing this direction was an easy way to meet the school expectations for action research as well as continuing with the practice of using Essential Questions as required by the school district. Honestly, we wanted something "easy" to start the year off and get us going.

For this cycle, we focused on those Essential Questions related to con-tent area comprehension. As we formulated the questions we used Bloom's Taxonomy to ensure different content areas used questions with comparable

Table 7.1 Writing Rubric

Name:
Date Submitted:

Teacher:
Title of Work:

Criteria	1	2	3	4	Points
Organization	Sequence of information is difficult to follow.	Reader has difficulty following work because student jumps around.	Student presents information in logical sequence that reader can follow.	Information in logical, interesting sequence that reader can follow.	
Content Knowledge	Student does not have grasp of information; student cannot answer questions about subject.	Student is becoming comfortable with content and is able to demonstrate basic concepts.	Student is at ease with basic content, but fails to elaborate.	Student demonstrates full knowledge (more than required).	
Grammar and Spelling	Work has four or more spelling errors and/or grammatical errors.	Presentation has three misspellings and/or grammatical errors.	Presentation has no more than two misspellings and/or grammatical errors.	Presentation has no misspellings or grammatical errors.	
Neatness	Work is illegible.	Work has three or four areas that are sloppy.	Work has one or two areas that are sloppy.	Work is neatly done.	
References	Work displays no references.	Work does not have the appropriate number of required references.	Reference section was completed incorrectly.	Work displays the correct number of references, written correctly.	
				TOTAL	

Adapted from: http://www.teach-nology.com/cgi-bin/writing.cgi.

Teacher Comments:

levels of thinking. By designing a standard writing rubric (table 7.1) across all classes, we hoped to compare scores and show progress.

Over the first quarter our students improved 10 percent between pre- and post-test rubric scores. Although we had considered this our easy way out, we were pleasantly surprised with the progress and decided to continue on through second quarter with a similar goal. We examined our strategies, expectations, and data in order to plan ways to assist our students in their continuing improvement.

At this point each content area teacher agreed to check the research in order to bring new ideas to the table. Suggestions ranged from offering the students peppermints while working (shown to help concentration), to scaffolding student writing, to defining expectations clearly in each classroom. There was no strategy we weren't willing to implement in order to increase student achievement.

REALIZING THE VALUE OF TEAMWORK

Around that time our principal also introduced a new piece of professional development software: *PD-360.* I admit my first thought was, "What now?" However, as soon as I began to utilize it, I knew the value. No longer would my team have to search and search for new strategies—they were all right there! I began finding and sharing short videos with my team, and while we didn't always agree on the value of each strategy, we were all focused on the same goal for the first time. By the end of second quarter our students' comprehension, as evaluated by our Essential Question rubrics, had increased another 6 percent.

We knew the third quarter (including FCAT testing) would be difficult. As an eighth grade team, we would be testing with our students five times in the next nine weeks. We all felt the pressure for our students to succeed, the demands of student discipline this quarter, and the added expectations of action research.

Fortunately, our language arts teacher came to one of our action research meetings with information she had gathered from the FCAT Writes pre-test. She was concerned that our students could not effectively compose short or extended response answers. Other team teachers agreed that the students were challenged to answer essay questions with fluency and organization.

We began to look at ways to improve students' essay writing and incorporated this goal into our action research learning cycle for that quarter. Our early discussions focused on what aspects of the students' writing concerned us. Our language arts teacher was vital in these conversations, paraphrasing our concerns in academic language. She noted most of our students were answering questions using clauses instead of more complex sentences and even paragraphs. We set out to instruct our students on the difference and hoped that this explicit instruction would help improve their writing.

We also put together a short checklist so that the students would understand the expectations (table 7.2). We created posters for each classroom and individual copies for each student to refer to as needed. After a few weeks we began seeing improvements in written answers as the students used these tools. All the teachers began to get the overall feeling of, "They're getting it!"

At the beginning of this learning cycle only 53 percent of our students wrote short response answers we considered worthy of the full two points on the FCAT grading scale. By the end of the quarter 67 percent of our students wrote acceptable answers for full credit. We were more than pleased with the overall increase in performance, especially considering these results came after just one quarter of concerted team effort.

REFLECTING BACK

And now here I sit, writing this chapter for our action research book—on maternity leave! My team and I have been corresponding about our focus for the fourth quarter. Of course the language arts teacher, so pleased with the students' progress, wants to push on with their writing. Another teacher on my team has brought to our attention that our students struggle with what to include in content area note-taking. As we get more accustomed to the action research cycle and continue seeing such great results from our hard work, it all becomes worth it!

Table 7.2   Response Checklist

Response Checklist
☐ My response begins by re-phrasing the question into an answer.
☐ There are no run-on sentences or fragments/incomplete thoughts.
☐ I use important details from the text to support my answer.
☐ I paraphrase and use my own words to answer the questions.
☐ There is variety in the way my sentences begin.
☐ My response is clear, and it is easy to understand the meaning of my words.

If I could offer just one suggestion to anyone embarking on action research, I would suggest that you focus on what you do every day. Assess the strengths and the weaknesses of your students, decide what they need help with, and develop an action research goal. No one is asking you to add a ton of work to your already filled days. Just rearrange some time, combine some tasks, and through collaboration you will learn to use your time more effectively to accelerate your students' achievement!

EDITORS' DISCUSSION

Wow! Changing the habits of a professional lifetime is never easy. Danielle Lawrence typifies the resistance that most of us feel when asked to do something differently. She shares important insights through her account. The teachers on Danielle's team began this process only because the administration directed them to do so, but this teaching team was "pleasantly surprised" and came to value the collegiality and results of their efforts.

Danielle confirms that using action research to establish a culture of inquiry is not something done in addition to existing teacher responsibilities. It isn't just another thing teachers are asked to do! Authentic inquiry in Danielle's learning community was a catalyst to a more efficient use of time, more effective communication that would have been needed in any case, and accelerated results for the teachers and students. It did not require midnight oil and every other Saturday!

This chapter is a helpful example of how an interdisciplinary team, including a special education teacher, came together to be collaborative around a common goal. With secondary education departmentalized and working in "silos," structures that encourage looping and cross-curricular teaching should be studied and more widely considered. Perhaps teachers and administrators reading this book will be motivated to study these kinds of ventures themselves!

8

Write-On

Using Research Data to Improve Student Achievement

Karen Zantop

Facing a decline in students' state assessed writing performance, Karen Zantop leads a team that uses standardized test data as a starting point for overall improvement in student writing. The results of their action research informed the practices of the entire faculty.

Most school years begin with a routine of committees and meetings to assess what is best for our students and our school as a whole. Not this year! While the goals were the same, this year the talk was all action research. Having been introduced to this new approach, the question on most of our minds was "What now?" Was this just another gimmick thought up by some company to make a lot of money and a name for themselves? Let's face it, teachers have seen fads come and go. Does action research work? Has it been effective in helping students excel?

We didn't know but ventured as requested further into this unknown territory. Managing a school from a model using teacher research to promote student success was an interesting idea. After a visit from two colleagues at the University of South Florida (USF), we were off and running.

A DIFFERENT APPROACH

When using action research, teachers don't form a committee in the traditional sense and decide what type of research to explore. Rather, they discern what the particular needs are for the student population and proceed with the action research process. In our case the language arts teachers quickly identified an area of student need. Our school's writing scores on the Florida

Comprehensive Achievement Test (FCAT) had begun to fall over several years and from a 3.8 to a 3.7 (on a 1.0 to 6.0 scale) in the previous year. As a result, we lost our "A" school rating.

If this score truly reflected a decline in our students' ability to write effectively, then someone needed to take a look at the situation and take action to promote better writing practices schoolwide. Several brave language arts teachers decided to take on this formidable task. Action research as we would come to know it had begun. This is a story of how our school went from an average school score of 3.7 to 4.4 on the FCAT Writes in just three years.

Facilitating the Group Dynamics

As our first meeting approached, I was apprehensive about the direction of the work. I knew where we wanted to end up, but getting there, the unknown, was unsettling. At our first meeting there was some discussion about who would lead the group as a group, but I was asked to take this role. In reality, everyone had their part and everyone had their say. My job as facilitator was to keep the group on track.

I was soon to realize this was an important and challenging job. This group was quite fluid in nature. There was a core of language arts teachers and the principal, but as we needed more information or particular skills, we would reach out to others. This flexible approach worked for us because as we moved in different directions, interest and talent played a role. At certain times, we would request that a colleague join us to provide us with their particular expertise and guidance.

The action research writing committee met formally every few weeks, as we knew time was of the essence and all the teachers needed this information. Our goal was to boost the students' writing abilities. To begin, we brainstormed the practices that we thought beneficial and important to the teaching of writing.

We got off to a slow start because so many ideas were being promoted and not surprisingly different committee members thought their different ideas should be chosen for use across the school. All kidding aside, I knew my ideas were *really* the best! Actually there were many well-thought-out ideas for schoolwide writing improvement blossoming all around us.

There were some skeptics, teachers who questioned this exercise and suggested that we should simply follow the curricular text on test preparation. We understood their point, but action research means exploring *all* the possibilities. To support the academic aspect of teaching writing, we explored ways to promote excellence and personal roles and responsibilities as we considered a variety of methods. These included creating incentives for students such as a pool/pizza party at the YMCA and the opportunity to change places with the principal for a day for students who attained perfect scores.

Planning Our Work Together

During the first year we created a scope and sequence for our middle school that teachers could use vertically across the grade levels so that there was a systematic development of writing skills. This was a new direction for us and led to some earnest conversations among the eight language arts teachers, each of whom had strong opinions. Fortunately we received invaluable support as the school district implemented curriculum mapping for all subject areas.

Armed with these materials, the group created posters to foster good writing. The sixth grade teachers took responsibility and designed "Topic, Audience, Purpose, Plan" (TAPP) posters. These were created to focus the students on important aspects of the writing process and were made available to each classroom in the school.

To assist our action research, our group believed a visit to another school would help us research successful techniques for the writing process. Our neighboring middle school's students had scored the highest in the county for several years, and we wanted to see if any of their strategies could be used to improve our students' writing abilities. After the visit, we decided to adopt some new strategies.

Firstly, it seemed imperative that we have a schoolwide writing practice day so that students in every grade would get some early feedback on their own achievement level. The practice writing day went well, so we proceeded to add a practice writing for all sixth and seventh grades while the eighth grades sat for the FCAT writing test. We hoped that this experience would serve the younger students well, and within three years our school writing score was an average 4.3.

Several factors could have influenced these scores, but we continue to use and build on the practices we discovered through our action research. Dividing up this work was easy as every teacher volunteered to do their share. One teacher was responsible for creating the practice test for the sixth and seventh graders. This was a complex job, but the teacher was willing to take it on. All teachers were given the test and answer key so they could work with their assigned students.

We did confront some problems with this type of planning and these types of activities. There was some irregularity in the grading as teachers responded to the writing in different ways, and some students did not get a final score. Sadly, those students felt left out. We wondered whether for some teachers grading represented too much extra work, so we knew that the next time we would need to plan to enlist the help of other colleagues such as assistant principals and the reading specialist.

Reaching Individual Students through Conferencing

The action research committee also recommended the school obtain substitutes for the eighth grade teachers prior to the FCAT Writing test. This allowed the teachers to work one-on-one with each student, who now received personalized tutoring on his or her writing. I had the opportunity to observe and conference with students, and they greatly appreciated the effort and were motivated in their writing endeavors. They listened intently and appreciated each suggestion and saw how their scores were improving.

We relied upon ourselves to make this task manageable for all students. We came up with a list of "must dos" to augment the scheduled writing classes. We required each student to write a minimum of 350 words so that their stories had sufficient interest and detail. Using the state scoring rubric to guide students, they were then coached to go back and use more descriptive vocabulary. Techniques such as projecting into the future to create the best conclusion proved extremely effective.

Of all the strategies we tried, the action research committee found the days given to individual conferencing to be a powerful strategy. We believe there is nothing better than giving students personal positive and corrective feedback on their writing samples. As a result of our observations of the process, a best practices list was compiled and distributed to all our colleagues, and the entire staff have responded by including these ideas in their lessons.

We were pleased at how many teachers stepped in to grade practice essays. Our principal, assistant principals, reading specialist, and others took on this job with enthusiasm! Attention to writing had reached an all-time high, and all that was left was to wait "impatiently" for the results.

THE RESULTS OF THE WRITING EMPHASIS

At long last and after a school year of action research, the scores were in, and we met our goal of improving student writing. Originally, we had planned that the principal would shadow anyone who earned a top score of six on the test. To our delight, SSMS students received so many perfect scores that this was impossible. Instead our principal agreed to sit on the roof all day to celebrate the success of our eighth graders, to the delight of *all* our students.

After the students received their scores, the committee agreed to survey them on how they were able to improve the overall quality of their writing. We realized that our students had made great strides in their ability to write, and we would only have this short window of opportunity at the end of the year to pick their brains about how they perceived the writing process and instruction. We asked them three simple questions:

- What writing technique did you use while taking the FCAT Writing test that you feel helped your score?
- Had you ever used this technique before?
- What did you learn in your class this year that helped you to become a better writer?

Students responded that the individual conferences, the "No Dead Verbs" lesson, the formal essay training, and *Caught'ya! Grammar with a Giggle* (by Jane Keister, 2003) were their favorites. They also noted critical techniques such as planning tools, enhancing vocabulary, and focusing on topic. They reported that they felt intelligent, capable, and empowered to become better writers and felt prepared to respond on the state's formal writing assessment. We summarized the results and sent them to the faculty. The state writing scores that followed our research and implementation were indeed impressive, and we felt our time spent on research was beneficial. The writing scores are shown in table 8.1.

Our writing action research group continued to serve as a resource during the next school year (2006–2007). We didn't want to lose the gains from the teachers' and students' hard work. Staff members continued to be aware of and

Table 8.1   Student Writing Scores

Academic Year	Percent of Students Testing at the Passing Score of 3.5 or Above
2005	71% (The year we lost our "A" rating.) We began our action research in fall 2005.
2006	86% (The next school year a new middle school opened and took a significant amount of our lower socioeconomic population.)
2007	91%
2008	93%

use our strategies. The school score continued to increase as we continued to implement the great practices that resulted from our action research. We understand that any one action research initiative doesn't last forever, and as we respond to student needs, there may come a time for a commonsense conclusion, but for now we continue to research and implement effective practices.

The reader can be left with two important thoughts. With focused preparation and instruction students have the ability to write in an organized and creative manner. Action research helped us to create some basic guidelines and lesson plans to achieve the desired results of boosting the writing skills and scores of our eighth grade student body. Our research on writing strategies is ongoing. We have moved from our original research to include new techniques. In the end we had a dedicated group of motivated educators who believed in our students and their ability to rise to our writing expectations.

EDITORS' DISCUSSION

How do learning communities and action research co-exist with the pressures associated in this age of accountability and standardized tests? We were delighted that Karen Zantop wrote this vignette because it is heavily grounded in the realities of teaching today. In many ways this is an uncomplicated initiative, and perhaps the one some teachers relate to the most given the present educational climate. Karen's account allows teachers to think about how they may reconcile accountability requirements with professionally enriching activities.

We appreciate that this is a very real balancing act for many teachers, and this story represents one possible answer to our question. We often hear teachers say that they aren't allowed to deviate from prescribed methodologies when delivering the curriculum. This teaching team worked with their administration to identify resources to support student conferencing, and Karen's description of their experiences tells us that teachers can find ways to enrich a prescribed curriculum.

This account also highlights another benefit of the learning community. Karen points out the irregularities in grading that surfaced when the teachers on her team came together to discuss their assessments. This is one example of how teachers can discover inconsistencies when they work together, and then help one another to find consistencies and other solutions. When variations in our practice are revealed, we can talk through our teaching behaviors and the strategies that work.

9

Action Research

Motivating Middle School Students

Karen Wood

Karen Wood with help from René Howery shares an example of action research across two school sites. They were particularly interested in how to reach children who were seemingly unmotivated to reach their potential. In this account they targeted a specific group of underachieving sixth graders and planned deliberate strategies that invited the children into the learning process.

As a veteran teacher, one of the most frustrating aspects of my job is watching very talented and intelligent students flounder and fail. Somewhere along the way, getting a good education and experiencing the joy of learning something new have been lost on these students. What causes this? What can I do to turn them around? These are the questions I struggled with year after year. As our school delved into action research schoolwide, I decided this process might hold the answer to my dilemma and frequent source of frustration!

STARTING WITH THE RESEARCH

I began my research by Googling "motivating middle school students." Many links to articles and books on the subject were readily available. Each evening I printed and read an article or two. There were many educators with the same concerns I had, and they were more than happy to share their thoughts and strategies! After reading several articles, I contacted a math teacher, René Howery, from River Ridge Middle School. I told her about the articles I had been reading and what experts say about unmotivated students. She and I had previously worked together at Seven Springs Middle School (SSMS) and had many discussions about students who seemingly "choose" to fail.

I invited René to join me on my journey to use the action research process to find answers to my questions. We met for a few hours and decided data from two different school populations might help us find solutions that would be more reliable.

René and I began reading the articles together and ordered numerous books that would help us use some "tried and true" strategies. We gathered academic achievement data throughout the first quarter on any student on our teams failing more than one subject. We researched their previous Florida Comprehensive Achievement Test (FCAT) Math and Reading levels.

Our goal was to compare each student's ability level to their standardized performance level. We checked previous years' scores and grades to determine if there was an established pattern for each student or if this was a recent development. We believed understanding these patterns would be an integral part of solving the problem for each student. The books we read included:

- Mender, A., *Motivating Students Who Don't Care.*
- Bruns, J. H., *They Can But They Don't: Helping Students Overcome Work Inhibition.*
- Rimm, S., *Why Bright Kids Get Poor Grades.*
- Smith-Rex, S., and Rex, J., *101 Creative Strategies for Reaching Unmotivated Learners.*
- Theobald, M., *Increasing Student Motivation: Strategies for Middle School and High School Students.*

In addition to these books, we read several articles by Mike Muir from the *Journal of the Maine Association for Middle Level Education.* We discussed each of the strategies and suggestions offered by these authors and looked for commonality among them as a starting point.

CHOOSING OUR STRATEGIES

The two strategies we tried—making work more interesting to the students and showing a personal interest in the students—laid the foundation for our work. Our students completed an "Interest Inventory." Based on the responses we created assignments that utilized the students' areas of interest, such as a sports theme throughout football season and baseball during the World Series.

We also took advantage of any opportunity to make positive, personal comments to those who were failing multiple classes. Comments offered academic support as students entered or exited our classrooms and as we walked around the class during lessons, and personal encouragement outside of class when we saw them in the hallways. Personal comments could be as simple as "I love your new haircut!" Some of the students responded positively to this personal attention and began working harder in our classes.

Report card data gathered at the end of first quarter was somewhat encouraging, but we each had a number of students earning math grades that were lower than their indicated abilities. Some of these students had frequent absences and missed assignments that contributed to their low grades. We continued reading the books on our list.

The next strategy we incorporated was "choice." Researchers reported that students were often more willing to work for teachers who gave them choices in projects, written assignments, and required reading. We decided we could incorporate choices in our classes each week. Students were sometimes allowed to do either odd or even problems from textbook assignments as long as they completed the correct number of assigned problems. These students knew the answers to the odd problems were in the back of the book and were amazed that we were willing to allow them to do these problems as long as their work was shown alongside the answer.

We also gave tests and quizzes with more problems than normal and instructed the class to choose a designated number of problems to answer. The majority of the students in each class often performed better on these assessments.

Further, the targeted students were allowed to choose their seats in our classrooms as long as they made sure there were focused and hardworking students nearby. By the time we allowed this, they were well aware of which classmates would have a positive impact and influence on them.

The targeted students soon realized these other students offered an additional opportunity for help and support. Part of our daily routine included discussing problems with a collaborative partner. Students were directed to discuss solutions with someone to their left, right, in front of them, or behind them. So at some point, they discussed problems and solutions with higher-performing students.

Seeking Guidance from the Guidance Counselor

In his book *They Can But They Don't*, Jerome Bruns (1992) indicated that disengaged, unmotivated students could be successful academically if they were part of a small guidance group. He stated that middle school students often needed to participate for at least six months in one of these groups in order to begin to make gains. I persuaded the sixth grade guidance counselor to help select ten students on my team who were in the greatest danger of failing multiple classes.

We planned to meet with the group once a week for thirty minutes for the rest of the school year. Our main goal was to offer these students the individual attention they needed and to help equip them with the confidence in themselves that they were lacking. In our first session the students made an origami cube. They wrote a list of "speed bumps" that kept them from being successful in the classes they were failing and put the list inside their cube. The cubes were then displayed on the top shelf of a bookcase until our last session.

All of the activities were structured in a way that required each student to be respectful of everyone else and to listen carefully. Many of them found this challenging and needed frequent reminders not to interrupt others. Eventually, we initiated a system with "chips" that could be "cashed in" when it was their turn to talk about that week's topic. Once they had "spent their chip" they could not contribute again until everyone else had had a turn to talk. The topics ranged from how they had achieved success in school in the past, to goals they could set to be sure to stay on track in the future.

We discovered each of these students was lacking social skills necessary to be successful in classrooms and school settings. Several of them lacked the confidence to volunteer or speak out in class. However, in the small group setting, they became more comfortable with one another and were able to contribute to our weekly discussions. They began to see how their peers affected them in and out of class.

Six of the ten students requested a seating change in math class for the fourth quarter so they could better focus. This was certainly a positive sign of growing maturity and an appreciation of the small group guidance work. They understood that they were capable of doing all the assigned work and that many times it was just a matter of self-confidence and prioritizing their time outside of class.

When we met for the last time the students opened their cubes from the beginning of the semester and read their list. A couple of them commented, "Oh, I'm not doing that anymore!" None of these students failed math that year and, furthermore, none of them failed more than one class either. This was a tremendous improvement from where they began in January.

OUR REFLECTIONS ON THIS ACTION RESEARCH EXPERIENCE

I do not believe students want to fail and set out to do so on purpose. I believe each student needs to know there are significant people in their lives who are listening to them, who care about what happens to them each day, and who are willing to forgive them when they take a few steps backward.

Teachers must not give up on these students but must help them begin each new day as an opportunity to become more responsible for their own successes. We must convince them there is great value in becoming lifelong learners and that's what all of us truly should be. Probably the most powerful discovery these students made was that being smart and capable is only a small part of being successful. Work ethic proved to be a much stronger indicator of success in any given class.

René and I agreed the changes we made in our classrooms based on the research last year were beneficial to all our students and well worth repeating. We will continue these strategies to impact the approximately 10 percent of our student populations who seem to have given up on themselves. None of these changes cost us any additional money in our budgets. They did not require us to adopt totally new teaching styles. The amount of additional planning time was actually minimal and barely impacted our normal schedules. Most days it was just a matter of thinking from our students' point of view about what would make learning more exciting and interesting.

We continued to teach our normal math curriculum but found better ways to increase the relevancy of our content, resulting in struggling students becoming more actively engaged in their own learning.

EDITORS' DISCUSSION

Karen Wood's story reflects a struggle that many veteran teachers experience. What is the key to motivating students who seem to have lost their way in the system? Karen and her colleague René Howery collaborated to find some answers to their dilemma by taking a concrete approach that illustrates one possible starting point in the action research process for many educators. They read research, identified strategies, put them into practice, collected data, and reflected on the results. A classic action research cycle! This piece teaches us that using the process of action research brings targeted strategies to the forefront of the teachers' consciousness for a true analysis of impact.

This very action enables professionals to determine whether strategies are truly impacting students or should be abandoned for what does work. For staff developers and administrators, this example is a powerful insight into how strategies, when addressed through this process, can truly become embedded in teacher practice—a missing link with which our profession has wrestled for years! Another interesting aspect of this story is the collaboration of Karen and René, which occurred across schools. This represents one more way to enrich the action research cycle and think about the possibilities of building community across a district.

Finally, the practicality of Karen and René's work should be noted. Student motivation is at the very heart of academic success and effective teaching. It is one of the great challenges facing every teacher, and yet these two teachers didn't hesitate to address the issue. René and Karen were undaunted and approached their research in a straightforward manner, and were able to tackle this perpetual concern for most teachers within the context of their own schools.

REFERENCES

Mender, A. (2000). *Motivating Students Who Don't Care: Successful Techniques for Educators.* Bloomington, IN: National Educational Service.

Bruns, J. H. (1992). *They Can But They Don't: Helping Students Overcome Work Inhibition.* New York, NY: Penguin Books USA, Inc.

Rimm, S. (1995). *Why Bright Kids Get Poor Grades and What You Can Do About It: A Six Step Program for Parents and Teachers.* New York, NY: Three Rivers Press.

Smith-Rex, S., and Rex, J. (2005). *101 Creative Strategies for Reaching Unmotivated Learners.* Chapin, SC: YouthLight, Inc.

Theobald, M. A. (2006). *Increasing Student Motivation: Strategies for Middle School and High School Students.* Thousand Oaks, CA: Corwin Press.

10

A Splash of Color with a Dash of Discovery Makes One Great Shade

Lisa Fisher

In this chapter Lisa Fisher describes her action research into the role of color in her classroom. She describes the action process from her first ideas, the research she found on the subject, the changes she made in her classroom and in her delivery of the curriculum, and the results she saw from this initiative. In her summary she shares a few ideas on her action research with a "Splash of Color."

I have a teacher friend who continuously expresses frustration with her middle school students' inability to understand what she explains. "I say it five times," she laments, yet the students still raise their hands and say, "I don't understand; what are we supposed to do?" I empathize with her frustration, then we always part with the same conclusion, "I will just explain the concepts slower so they will get it and not have to ask me over and over to explain it again, right?" This is more of a question than a statement. We both know this is not the answer to our problem, so what is the solution?

Every teacher wants to see his or her students succeed on some level, but to yield such results, teachers must continuously observe, reflect, and revise their teaching in order to meet the learning needs of their growing students in a changing society. "Teachers throughout the world are developing professionally by becoming teacher-researchers, a wonderful new breed of artists-in-residence" (Hubbard & Power, 2003, xiii) who take this historical process and invite the students to be collaborators within the world of learning. This process can easily occur through the implementation of action research.

THE BURST OF BRILLIANT DEPTH

Last year, I noticed my sixth grade reading students and my seventh and eighth grade intensive reading students had difficulty reading to learn new information. This prompted me to analyze my own ability to read to learn since I was finishing up my master's degree. I thought about my personal use of highlighters and color pens; I used color pens to organize my class notes and highlighters to mark key points within texts. I also had a color system for proofreading. Color allowed my mind to visualize where information was located on a page and string that information into meaningful definitions and explanations and transfer it to my long-term memory.

At the completion of my degree, I decided the use of color had to be part of the reason for my academic success. I thought the use of color could also help younger students make achievement gains across content areas. That is when it happened—the question that ignited a fire within my mind. *Will the use of color help students improve academically and increase retention and comprehension of new material across content areas?* It was not the whole idea, but it was a start. As e. e. cummings reminds us, "Always the more beautiful answer who asks the more beautiful question" (quoted in Sawyer-Laucanno, 2004, 418).

Unfortunately, the school year ended with just that, a question. In all my years of being a student in school, I had never read any research on this newfound interest of mine, and I was not even certain research existed to support my theory. How would I get my principal, Mr. Christoff, to support me in finding the answer to my question? Then I remembered what Albert Einstein said, "If we knew what it was we were doing, it would not be called research, would it?" (quoted in Thorpe, 2000, 47).

Therefore, I did what any well-respected teacher with a crazy new idea would do; I went to Mr. Christoff, principal of Seven Springs Middle school, and nervously explained that I wanted to do research on how color helps students increase reading comprehension and asked if it would be acceptable to paint my classroom. Mr. Christoff responded that if I did the research and the color was not too outrageous, I could do it. I was so excited and overwhelmed at the same time. All I could think about was where to start and how to get there.

THE COLORFUL DESIGN

With two months of summer break staring me in the face, I started by creating a plan that would elicit an answer to my question and possibly open doors to new unconsidered questions. My first step was to locate as much research on the topic as possible and read and evaluate the data; I knew I needed to create a method of instruction for the classroom (model and practice) and find a way to test my question in order to get results. According to Hubbard and Power (2003):

> The design is a way of formalizing your intention to dig deeper into one question or one piece of your curiosity about teaching and your students. And like every aspect of the research project, the design will continue to evolve in large and small ways once you begin to collect and analyze data. (28)

The school district's online resource helped me locate multiple articles on the topic of the use of color with students. Some of the articles were just opinion pieces, and some were irrelevant to the angle I was trying to approach. I felt some frustration as I must have read about twenty articles before I finally came across one that described a research process with the use of color. Fortunately, I ended up finding a total of five articles that represented research, and I held on to all the others just in case I needed them.

The research about color varied across grade levels and approaches. Research states:

- Use of colorful visual images compared to black and white suggests that colorful images increase the level of learning when applied to specified tasks (Worley & Moore, 2001).
- Color is a factor in visual memory (Spence, Wong, Rusan, & Rastegar, 2005).
- Colors in a classroom can affect how students behave and perform (Kennedy, 2005).
- Increased school pride and decreased behavior problems, including vandalism, occurs in schools that make color changes (Thompson, 2003).
- The use of color in the classroom is an effective method for promoting faster development and increased motivation in students (Baird, 2006).

Once I spent about a month reading and evaluating all the research similar to my topic of interest, more questions emerged such as, Will the use of color help all types of learners? Will certain colors in the environment aid the stimulation of learning? Can the use of color help students improve achievement in all classes? In what ways should color be used? How can it be adapted to fit the needs of all teachers and students?

It was then I realized this action research was bigger than me. I was going to need to talk my teammates into taking on part of the process as a possible learning cycle goal so I could get the answers to my questions that reached beyond my classroom walls.

Gaining Support from Administration

Sharing my newfound interest with the entire school would provide school-wide feedback on the implementation, students' acceptance, and usefulness of color in the classroom with students from different grade levels. There-fore, in the midst of summer, I e-mailed Mr. Christoff, asking if I could give a presentation on how color can enhance learning in the classroom at a Lunch & Learn this coming year.

He agreed, suggesting I share the research sometime during September or October so teachers could use the information early enough in the year to ob-serve the effectiveness. How lucky I was to work at a school with a principal who not only talks about, but also promotes, the "process" of action research.

I impatiently awaited Mr. Christoff's approval of the paint color for the walls. I chose a color called Hark-a-way (a light green with a hint of blue tone) and the best time to get into my classroom to actually paint the walls. Green/blue tones promote calm behavior among secondary students (Ken-nedy, 2005). I was able paint my classroom the week before teacher planning week. Boy, was I excited! Now, with the research and painting out of the way, I was able to focus on the next step—deciding how and when to collect the necessary data from my students, teammates, and colleagues.

SHADES OF COLLECTION

During teacher planning week, my teammates and I sat down together to iron out the details for the start of the school year. I told them I had an idea for our first learning/action research cycle that would benefit all of our subject areas. I explained my summer research and asked them if they wanted to do it with me.

I could see my teammates mulling it over in their minds. "What would we have to do?" one of them asked hesitantly, which I could understand because research is time-consuming and they do have their own agenda to teach. I de-scribed the need to give the students a pre-test related to our specific classes and determine the mean from each period and then the average overall.

Next, we would model the use of color and allow students to practice the use of color over a few months and provide a visual for them to refer to, like a poster. Finally, we would give our students one post-test without the use of color and one with the use of color to determine if it appeared to influence students' academic achievement.

My teammates had questions. They wondered where the pre-test would come from for each of their subject areas and how they would learn about the color coding. I explained that we would create our own test items and that I would demonstrate a process I had designed for using color and give them a poster to keep in their classrooms. With that, they agreed to continue the conversation.

One week later, we all met back in my classroom. I gave a presentation to guide my team and the Lunch & Learn colleagues on the use of color within the classroom in order to enhance students' understanding. I explained the details related to using color. Students would use highlighters or color pens, pencils, or markers to mark up text during reading or taking notes.

They would use only four colors (orange, green, blue, and pink) in order to keep it simple, and the same colors and similar system throughout all of their classes. For example, in reading, students would identify the topic or topic sentence/main idea of a text with orange; the descriptive words or supporting details with green; fact versus opinion in blue; and the author's purpose, tone, and/or emotional appeal in pink. When students were not permitted to write on the text, they used overhead transparencies or color sticky notes. The variation is not as important as the consistency.

Putting Our Plans into Action

In early August, I walked my teammates through the research, the benefits, the different ways to use color (textbooks, articles, and class notes), and data collection process. It felt gratifying to finally share my months of research. After the first and second team meeting discussing student data I sensed my teammates were not as excited about this research as I was. They seemed concerned about the extra work they were going to have to do. Nonetheless, I was hopeful that they would all begin the process using color within their classrooms.

Within two weeks we had our pre-test results for each of our content area classes. The pre-test was given to each student with the use of a pencil and without the use of color. The pre-test results based on the content to be covered in the first learning cycle for each of our content areas:

Geography	55%
Reading	67%
Language Arts	67%

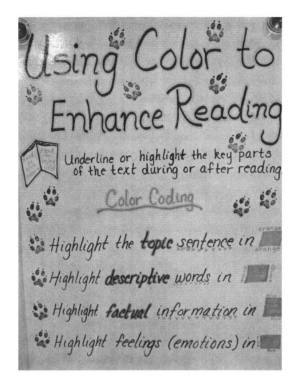

| Math | 44% |
| Science | 39% |

In addition to the pre-test, I also determined each student's learning style in my content area through a multiple intelligences assessment. We also observed our students' attitudes and moods as they implemented the color system. Each teacher on the team hung a poster in a central location so students could easily see the color chart. Figure 10.1 represents the poster that was displayed in the reading classroom for students to refer to as needed.

We walked the students through the use of colors (orange, green, blue, and pink) in their textbooks, class notes, and reading passages. Students were able to practice the use of color to enhance achievement/understanding on a regular basis.

We observed students using color in every class when taking notes as well as when they read. If we forgot to tell them to take out their highlighters, they would remind us. I was amazed at their enthusiasm. I have to laugh though, because usually when students are asked to turn to their class notes section of their binder I hear many gripes and moans, but this year I did not have that experience, which I can only attribute to the use of color.

The sharing continued after the Lunch & Learn presentation at SSMS. The graphic art teacher noted the students did like colored paper, colored markers, and colored pencils. She had begun to create handouts on colored paper and predicted this would improve the amount of homework being returned. She also stated it had helped with notebook checking because it was easy to ask for the green paper or the pink paper.

The science teacher at SSMS used color coding for students' notes. When teaching acids and bases, she asked the students to take notes on acids on the pink paper and write about bases on blue paper. They all got those questions correct on the quiz!

In my reading class, students were able to practice using color in a variety of ways. I felt confident my students were experiencing a strategy that could help them read to learn. However, I realized my theory was incomplete until we gave the post-test.

THE COLOR CRITIQUE

As the data came pouring in, I found myself elated by the numerical information. Questions began to arise out of the blue simply from analyzing the data. The students with a pre-test mean of 67 percent in reading scored 89 percent on the post-test. Unfortunately, some students moved away between tests so I tested seventy-one nonvisual/spatial learners for the pretest, but only tested sixty-nine nonvisual/spatial learners for the post-test. The visual/spatial learners made 18 percent gains and the nonvisual/spatial learners made 22 percent gains.

Therefore, the data reveals there is not a correlation between the use of color and learning style. I thought there would be. I learned research is not about proving yourself right, but finding out the best way to educate the students.

As a matter of fact, one student who demonstrated a 33 percent gain noted, "To me, using color was a fun way to organize my information. It made it easier to comprehend what I was learning because instead of just staring at a white piece of paper for thirty minutes attempting to study, I had color-coded notes that didn't hurt my eyes. I found that when using color, I did better on my tests." Another student stated, "I think color has really enhanced my learning experience. Seeing things in color, it seems more useful and easier to understand. When using color in my notes, I can organize it and look for something specific with ease."

Table 10.1   Content Area Pre-test and Post-test Scores

Content Area	Pre-test Score	Post-test Score	Percent Gain
Geography	55%	65%	10%
Reading	67%	88%	21%
Language Arts	67%	73%	6%
Math	44%	46%	2%
Science	39%	N/A	

The use of color in class notes and with text seems to be based on each student's personal preference. As one teammate, Melanie Bacca (math teacher), shared, "I found that the use of color helped several students, and they still use it today. [Although] some seemed not to benefit, I would definitely keep using it."

It was difficult to get the post-test results from *all* my team members, but most of them finally came through. I never received the post-test results from one teacher. Table 10.1 shows the pre-test and post-test scores across each content area.

The math scores were disappointing, but the math teacher reminded me of the difficulty some students have learning math with or without the use of color.

THE REVEAL

Perhaps using color-coding in text and/or with class notes and painting your classroom are not radical solutions for teaching and learning, but they certainly have sparked a positive attitude from the sixth grade students with whom we interact on a daily basis. One student commented, "I think using color helps bring life to the room, the notes, and the text," while another shared, "I love the color; it's cool and no other classes have color on the walls." Students also indicated they wanted to be in the classroom and made comments such as, "It is nicer to be in this room because it feels cozier." Another positive impact was a decrease in classroom referrals. During the previous year, I had written eight referrals, but this year I only wrote four referrals. So was it worth the time I spent painting? I think so!

In conclusion, I believe students responded positively to the use of color and being surrounded by color. While not all students showed improvement from the pre-test to the post-test, I suggest the use of color should still be taught. Teachers and students will make the final decision as to whether they are going to use it, just like they do with strategies and graphic organizers.

Color is one of many tools teachers can utilize to inspire students to grasp learning from a different perspective. Who knows? This just might be the colorful makeover your struggling learners have been searching for.

When you walk into a room and are surrounded by massive white walls staring you down, you tend to feel the need to create an inviting atmosphere for learning. Consider the following before using color to influence learning. Through my action research I would suggest the following tips.

- Be sure to read the research on theories about reactions to different colors. For example, you would not want to paint your classroom red or put an assignment on red paper. Nor would you want to use primary colors in a secondary classroom. It's not cool!
- Make sure you check with your school principal before you paint your classroom. Have a paint color ready to show him or her, and have a purpose for painting your classroom. Simply to add décor to the environment is not enough of a reason!
- Have a plan for the use of color. Don't just tell students to use color because they will highlight or underline everything. You need to show what colors to use, how to use them, when to use them, and why the students should use them.
- Pick a limited number of colors. I found my students did not remember the purpose of more than five colors. The reason for using color is to provide students with a strategy that will enhance understanding, so don't overdo it!
- Finally, if you work on teams at your school, have all the teachers use the same colors. This will ensure students don't have to have five different colors for each content class, and they are more likely to see the connections across curriculum due to the use of color.

These are just suggestions. You can choose to adjust the use of color to meet your classroom needs. Finally, keep in mind the journey does not stop here; action research is an ongoing process that must be constantly adapted over time.

EDITORS' DISCUSSION

The age of accountability is sometimes used as an excuse by some educators who claim to have no time to think about "extraneous" factors like the learning environment. It seems that every working hour must be dedicated to skills and content. Lisa Fisher reminds us that learning is stimulated by curiosity and can indeed be enhanced by ideas that may not occur to us at first glance when surrounded by a mountain of teacher's guides.

Without impacting the curriculum she was contracted to teach, Lisa studied and collected data about various techniques of applying color to the environment and integrating color into students' work. In the process, she learned about the use of color in ways she was able to share with her faculty and our readers.

The role of the administrator in this case should not be underestimated. While the principal encouraged Lisa to develop this line of inquiry, by asking her to share the results across the school faculty he simultaneously conferred legitimacy for this action research while implicitly expressing confidence in Lisa's capacity to complete her study successfully.

We see another lesson embedded in Lisa's account—that the action research process provides a way for teachers to test ideas that may not have been otherwise entertained. If teachers would like to lend credence to their ideas, posing their questions and initiating the collection and examination of data is a professional approach to testing hypotheses. This is a way to get to the bottom line—is this idea useful for students? All of us are feeling the pressure of time that must be maximized for student results. Action research can focus our efforts so we stay on track with what works.

REFERENCES

Baird, D. (January 2006). A Splash of Color, a Dash of Learning. *The Journal* 33(6): 38.

Hubbard, R. S., & Power, B. M. (2003). *The Art of Classroom Inquiry: A Handbook for Teacher-Researchers*. Portsmouth, NH: Heinemann.

Kennedy, M. (May 2005). Classroom Colors: The Hues You Choose for Classroom Furnishings Can Enhance a Student's Learning Environment. *American School & University* 77(10): 48–50.

Sawyer-Laucanno, C. (2004). *E. E. Cummings: A Biography*. Naperville, IL: Sourcebooks.

Spence, I., Wong, P., Rusan, M., & Rastegar, N. (2005). How Color Enhances Visual Memory for Natural Scenes. *Psychological Science Research Report*. 17 (1): 1–5.

Thompson, S. (December 2003). Color in Education. *School Planning & Management*. Retrieved from www.peterli.com/archive/spm/551.shtm.

Thorpe, S. (2000). *How to Think Like Einstein: Simple Ways to Break the Rules and Discover Your Hidden Genius*. Naperville, IL: Sourcebooks.

Worley, G., & Moore, D. (2001). The Effects of Highlight Color on Immediate Recall on Subjects of Different Cognitive Styles. *International Journal of Instructional Media*. 28(2): 169–179.

IV

AFFIRMING THE VOICE OF
THE TEACHER RESEARCHER

11

Reflecting Back on a Year of Growth

The Results of Thoughtful, Proactive, and Effective Teacher Research

Christine Crocco and Roger Brindley

> Teacher inquiry is a vehicle that can be used by teachers to untangle some of the complexities that occur in the profession, raise teachers' voices in discussions of educational reform, and ultimately transform assumptions about the teaching profession itself.
>
> —Nancy Dana and Diane Yendol-Hoppey,
> *The Reflective Educator's Guide to Classroom Research*

Seven Springs Middle School (SSMS), with its broad demographics, hardworking faculty, and strong administrative leaders, could be found across the United States—from Long Island, New York, to Long Beach, California, or any number of communities in between. What does differentiate this school is an action-oriented principal with teachers who trusted him enough to commit to a shared vision for their school. The teachers were willing to take a risk in a climate of accountability and begin the action research process, knowing that they would be supported in this situated and practical professional development.

In this book we featured the accounts of six inquiry-oriented teams on one school site, working as a professional community. Two of the vignettes (chapters 7 and 8) reflect teachers who are directly addressing student achievement on the Florida Comprehensive Achievement Test (FCAT). In chapters 6 and 9 the primary purpose of the teacher research was to target the specific needs of children, and chapters 5 and 10 illustrate the processes of action research. We believe there are important insights to be gained across these studies and share the lessons we have learned from this culture of inquiry.

RECOGNIZING THE PRACTICAL VALUE OF
ACTION RESEARCH ACROSS THE SCHOOL COMMUNITY

In chapter 5 Leslie Frick takes us through a twelve-month cycle from the wonderings that accompany the end of one school year as a teacher thinks to the future, to a point twelve months later where she reflects on the year that has been. Leslie allows us into her cognition as we read how she tried to find consensus with her team. We understand from her story that if members of a team can't see the value of the work, they will be hesitant to become involved.

A teacher's time is precious, so we must not just assume they want to be involved. The value of this work needs to be purposefully explained before teachers can be expected to make a commitment. For Leslie's colleagues it was appropriate for them to begin with individual goals. They needed to grow into this new sense of collaboration.

This complex work takes time and open communication skills, and school personnel may wish to seek support and even training. Leslie is honest about the ways she worked with her colleagues. She was persistent and proactive in seeking like-minded teachers. She put herself out there and learned that feeling a little vulnerable and taking risks can lead to more collaborative interactions. Leslie teaches us to celebrate the small victories along the way.

In the following chapter Cindy Tehan and Janet Tolson demonstrate the power of community ownership and the positive outcomes that result from involving their students in the curriculum. They describe focusing the energy and enthusiasm of their students around an issue of personal and communal importance. By illustrating in a very practical way the relevance of our communities and establishing a sense of stewardship for the environment, these two teachers allow students to experience success, take responsibility, and learn leadership skills.

This is a case of putting science into practice, a case of getting something done! Janet and Cindy describe a creative piece of research that inspired the children and resulted in a tangible and beneficial effect. It is, in a very real sense, "service learning" and begs the question, Why can't educators teach like this more often? This vignette confirms that if content is made relevant and *requires* the participation of students, the answer to the question above is, They can!

In the same way teachers empowered their students in this story, perhaps there is a parallel lesson for administrators seeking to empower teachers. Empowered teachers have the confidence to empower students. Empowering students or teachers is not an act of administrative abdication. Some administrators may fear they will lose control, when in fact they can act as a catalyst for teacher leadership. Similarly, teachers who empower students must continue to be responsible for their classroom cultures but can widen the possibilities of student learning as seen in Janet and Cindy's classroom and the ways in which they created an engaged community.

THE CHALLENGES OF
COLLABORATION AND ACCOUNTABILITY

Teachers coalescing around a goal is a messy business! Danielle Lawrence shares a very honest account of how teachers negotiated the critical processes associated with collaboration. Chapter 7 describes the first cautious steps in this process and shows how the initial results propelled the teachers to redouble their efforts, ultimately resulting in progress for their students.

Danielle's story ends with a teacher motivated to repeat the process the next school year and demonstrates how the inquiry cycle regenerates and establishes a more natural way of teachers working together. It shows how collaboration folds into everyday work. Teacher research is not just "one more thing to do"; rather it should be part of a teacher's daily practice. School-based research builds on itself over time, much like other forms of professional development; these behaviors can take several years to become internalized.

We advocate that teachers are careful how they incorporate inquiry into the curriculum. A few first cautious steps may allow teachers to gradually develop their capacity and to ultimately be successful. We share this thought aware of numerous initiatives or programs promoted as a "quick fix" or as "a solution" in recent years. Sadly, some of these so-called solutions were thrust upon teachers without the capacity building of job-embedded staff development.

If an inquiry approach to teaching is to improve practice, some teachers will need to take *gradual* developmental steps in a supportive culture. The alternative may be to constantly just start over with a new "fix" for the educational crisis du jour.

Karen Zantop's vignette reflects the realities of teaching in the age of accountability. In this case, writing teachers used the collaborative culture of their school and worked together to inform the critical prerequisite skills for successful middle school writers. They created a set of techniques for their students in an effort to ensure foundational skills prior to the standardized assessment. The focus is precise, the purpose is set, and the results can be clearly measured.

While advocates for professional learning communities or action research may encourage broader, perhaps loftier goals, this case speaks to the expectations of teaching in the present educational climate. We understand that we cannot ask teachers to adopt an inquiry orientation while ignoring the demands of accountability.

Karen's story confirms that action research can flourish in an era of contextual pressures associated with the collection of achievement data that must be systematically reported. It is also noteworthy that the teachers listened to and reflected on feedback from the students in this case. How nice that the students' feedback was valued! We leave Karen as she builds on this experience in her future teaching.

FROM STRAIGHTFORWARD TO OUT OF THE BOX!

In chapter 9, Karen Wood confirms that putting good ideas gleaned from professional readings into practice needs to be a deliberate act; it is not an accidental process or a haphazard act of osmosis! She recognizes and has written about this—student choice, open seating, interest inventories, and targeted guidance groups, to name a few strategies that as a veteran teacher she had prior knowledge of, but was now purposefully applying to meet specific needs in her classroom.

Karen's personal research has confirmed for her the "tried and true" strategies found in hundreds of professional books. She understood that she could read about "this stuff" all day long, but eventually she had to give herself permission to take a few modest risks. At one level these are just small incremental additions to her teaching. At another level, we see a veteran teacher encouraged to question and then adapt her teaching.

The support of her community and the structure of action research empowered her in-depth reflection. She noted the changes observed in some of her most at-risk students—seemingly small adjustments that made the difference between failure and success for them. For Karen, this inquiry allowed her to study these small adjustments. Unlike a workshop strategy taught in isolation, this job-embedded experience allowed her to internalize a set of strategies so they were truly a part of her ongoing practice.

Lisa Fisher reminds us that each one of us carries our own personal theories, and she described how, with the support of her administration, she set about testing *her* theory. She noted the frustration teachers feel when children aren't "getting it," and having read some supporting research, she set about answering her own question: Does color really make a difference? Cans of paint, use of color pens and coding systems, and lessons for her students on the psychological effects of different colors permeate her planning and teaching.

We may never know whether the increased student achievement is the result of other initiatives or Lisa's innovation around notions of color, or just a happy coincidence. That said—Lisa is convinced! She saw it in the intangibles—the faces and comments of her students. This is the case of how one teacher, soliciting the generous permission of her administration and colleagues, used action research to test out a theory.

As educators, we should all be prepared to test our personal theories and honestly appraise our findings. Lisa's story reminds us that when teachers have a deliberate and carefully thought-out plan, they should be encouraged to "color outside the lines." It also reinforces the art of teaching. Here is a teacher inspired by her passion to try something new. She was confident that her ideas had some merit, but she needed a framework to help put her plans into action and to give her ideas some professional credence.

It is also noteworthy that Lisa received support and encouragement from her administrator. If that administrator had cast dispersions on her initial ideas when she first went to him, she would not have been able to continue. This brings us nicely to the next key point.

THE CRITICAL ROLE OF A VISIONARY ADMINISTRATION

We have purposely left the administrators' chapter for last, as these teachers' vignettes could only have taken place with the guidance of the administrators. The principal and assistant principal envisioned and then created the structure for success. These administrators understood the role of scholarship in the culture of their school community. They recognized that in order for this initiative to be successful, they had to give teachers the skill sets, the structures, and, above all, permission to become researchers in their own right.

Chris Christoff and Matt Gruhl describe a very deliberate, developmental set of plans that they used to gradually create the space in which teachers began to become comfortable collaborating together. You can see from the Progress Update they share that every team was in its own developmental place. Some roared ahead; others were taking modest first steps. All were encouraged to share their learning and results and were provided the support they needed for their next steps.

Like so many other areas of teaching, some teams were more effective than others, but as long as the effort was authentic and documented, Chris and Matt met them where they were, provided feedback, and encouraged further development.

We wish to emphasize that at no time did these two administrators use their power to pass judgment on the teachers' proposals. How could they? They didn't know the outcomes ahead of time either. In fact, they were conducting their own administrative action research. They had done their own homework, set up their plans based upon their research, and collected their own data. Chris and Matt were learning about their own behaviors and adjusting their approach as they continued to move forward with supporting their teachers.

At times teams would negotiate new goals; at other times, they extended the existing work further. Over the course of two years, the teachers came to realize that they could trust their administration, that their peers trusted the administration too, and that the work was reinvigorating. As these efforts gained momentum, the process began to resemble the "flywheel" described by Collins (2001). SSMS was becoming a self-perpetuating culture of inquiry where the collective capacity allowed for a more enriched community for meeting the needs of the students.

For Chris and Matt, school leadership isn't about oversight or compliance; rather, it is about mentorship, modeling, and empowerment. As they created a shared vision with the teachers, they trusted the teachers would respond. In turn, the teachers came to view their administration as dedicated to resolving the contextual pressures of the school and worthy of their trust. The teachers came to realize that their administration viewed their collaborative inquiry process as essential to the success of the school.

SOME FINAL THOUGHTS

This book began with an overview of the two constructs that were prerequisites to the success of SSMS. The professional development outlined in the preceding chapters clearly does not occur in a vacuum. The administrators defined a structure and provided guidance for the teachers.

In learning about and then acting on the concepts of professional learning communities and action research, the administrators constructed a template for success that they believed would work at SSMS. They described a system that teachers could understand and begin to implement. As the teachers began to see the benefits of their situated learning, they were increasingly willing to reinvest their time and energy. These are simple descriptions of a complex phenomenon.

Yes, the work is messy and everyone is in a different place. This book confirms inquiry orientation as a developmental process. Everyone brings a different set of experiences and perspectives to the work. Some teachers will be cavalier, confident in their own experiences and skills and enter into action research with great gusto. Others will be reticent, with prior experiences that for whatever reason now make them hesitant. They will want to observe others go first. In reality most teachers probably fall in between these two cases.

What SSMS reminds us, above all else, is that teachers are central to the educative process. It will be the teacher in front of the classroom who will make or break the student experience every day. We believe that giving teachers the tools and respect to craft their professional work will positively impact our schoolchildren.

This professional learning community became a community of proactive engagement, a community of collegial support, and the teachers at SSMS felt a concentrated sense of belonging. They felt they had something different from other schools, something special and unique to themselves. All of this was possible because of an administration who were committed to the needs of the teachers and willing to use the concepts of professional learning communities and action research as a structure for increasing the collective capacity of the school.

The most important lesson we have learned is that educators can't wait for the perfect risk-free system. Reflective educators can adjust as they proceed. SSMS teaches all of us that the key is to BEGIN!

REFERENCES

Collins, J. (2001). *Good to Great: Why Some Companies Make the Leap . . . and Others Don't*. New York: HarperCollins Publishers.

Dana, N., & Yendol-Hoppey, D. (2009). *The Reflective Educator's Guide to Classroom Research: Learning to Teach and Teaching to Learn Through Practitioner Inquiry*. Thousand Oaks, CA: Corwin Press.

About the Editors

Roger Brindley is a professor and the interim associate director of USF World and the Patel Center for Global Solutions at the University of South Florida. Roger's research has focused on bridging theory and practice between the P–12 school and the university through studies on teacher beliefs and constructing professional development school partnerships. In 2009 Roger completed a four-year appointment as senior editor of *School-University Partnerships: The Journal of the National Association for Professional Development Schools.*

Roger believes master teachers have a remarkable set of skills, and his teaching and research is committed to extending effective pedagogy in teacher education. He was the 2003 recipient of the University of South Florida President's Award for Faculty Excellence. Roger loves to play soccer (however badly) and is grateful for his wife, Toni, and daughter, Kathleen.

Christine Crocco brings nineteen years of classroom teaching and over a decade of district office experience to her position as assistant director of the David C. Anchin Center at the University of South Florida (USF). Chris holds a B.A. in history from the University of Connecticut, an M.S. in language arts education from Eastern Connecticut State University, and earned her certification in Educational Leadership from USF.

She has worked extensively with teacher teams developing multiage learning environments. Chris is passionate about supporting administrators and teachers in creating the structures for job-embedded staff development. She attributes her early interest in teaching to her nine younger siblings! Chris draws strength from the love and support of her entire family—especially her husband, Danny.

About the Contributors

Christopher S. Christoff taught social studies at Seven Springs Middle School before being promoted to assistant principal in 2001 and then appointed principal in 2004. He received his bachelor's degree in social science education from the University of South Florida and his master's degree in educational leadership from National Louis University.

Chris has a strong belief in empowering teachers through the process of action research and working within professional learning communities. Chris is blessed with his wife, Christine, and two beautiful children, Christopher and Camryn. Chris is currently the principal of Crews Lake Middle School in Pasco County, Florida.

Lisa A. Fisher was a reading teacher and reading coach at Seven Springs Middle School. After graduating from the University of South Florida with a bachelor's degree in elementary education and a master's degree in reading education, Lisa is now a high school literacy coach. Lisa is a published author and an adjunct instructor for Pasco-Hernando Community College, where she teaches remedial reading courses for college-bound adults. Currently, Lisa resides in Land O' Lakes, Florida, where she enjoys life with her husband and four beautiful Chihuahuas (Zeus, Toby, Kiley Marie, and Lola).

Leslie Frick graduated from SUNY Brockport with a bachelor's degree in elementary education and history in 1990, and taught elementary school for eight years before becoming a middle school social studies and language arts teacher. In addition to her classroom responsibilities, Leslie trains new teachers in her district and developed programs assisting special needs students in the classroom and social settings. Leslie feels blessed to have enjoyed the last nineteen years with her husband, Steve, and their two sons, Tyler and Kyle.

Matthew Gruhl is currently the principal of Buffalo Creek Middle School in Manatee County, Florida. He earned his M.A. in social studies education and Ed.S. in educational leadership from the University of South Florida. Matt has been a teacher and an administrator at both the high school and middle school levels, and has a passion for helping teachers build true professional learning communities. Matthew draws strength and peace from his beautiful wife, Martye, and his two wonderful boys, Nathaniel and Stryker.

Danielle Lawrence is a middle school special education and reading teacher. She earned her B.A. in varying exceptionalities from the University of South Florida and is both reading and integrated curriculum certified. Acting as team leader alongside four other professionals, Danielle jumped into action research headfirst. However, teaching is only one of the hats she wears as she goes home to her husband, Jonny, and two children, Tyler and Avree.

Cynthia Tehan, a national board certified teacher, whose career spans more than thirty years, is currently teaching a leadership class and four classes of drama. She loves her job and is very proud of the teachers and administrators at Seven Springs Middle School. In March of 2009, SSMS was recognized as a Florida Learn and Serve Leader School—one of only two middle schools in the state. Cynthia loves to learn and is blessed with a loving husband and three accomplished daughters: Megan, Jenny, and Kelly.

Janet Tolson is a middle school reading teacher. She received her M.A. in reading and language arts education from the University of South Florida and has attained national certification as a middle childhood generalist. Janet continues to work with Ms. Tehan to promote service learning in education, and is also working with the National Youth Leadership Council as part of their generator schools network to support service learning nationally. She is grateful for the support and love from her son, Seattle.

Karen Wood teaches sixth grade math and is the math department chairperson at Seven Springs Middle School. She earned her B.S. degree from Georgia College in 1977 and has been teaching for thirty-two years. Karen is dedicated to helping math make sense to her students and helping them develop a love for learning math. She still gets excited when students begin asking more questions in an effort to improve their understanding of math concepts. She hopes her enthusiasm for math is contagious and her students will "catch" it!

Karen Zantop, a language arts teacher in Pasco County, is currently working with middle school students in the dropout prevention program. As a teacher for over twenty years, she is diligent in nurturing those children who "fall between the cracks" and continues to share successful language arts strategies with others. Karen is supported by her husband, Dan; three children; and three very active grandsons.

Breinigsville, PA USA
20 January 2011
253751BV00003B/5/P

9 781607 099673